MODERN WORLD NATIONS

England

Alan Allport

Series Consulting Editor
Charles F. Gritzner
South Dakota State University

CHELSEA HOUSE
PUBLISHERS
A Haights Cross Communications Company
Philadelphia

Frontispiece: Flag of England

Cover: Changing of the guard ceremony at Buckingham Palace.

CHELSEA HOUSE PUBLISHERS

VP, NEW PRODUCT DEVELOPMENT Sally Cheney
DIRECTOR OF PRODUCTION Kim Shinners
CREATIVE MANAGER Takeshi Takahashi
MANUFACTURING MANAGER Diann Grasse

Staff for ENGLAND

EDITOR Lee Marcott
PRODUCTION EDITOR Jaimie Winkler
PICTURE RESEARCHER Pat Holl
COVER AND SERIES DESIGNER Takeshi Takahashi
LAYOUT 21st Century Publishing and Communications, Inc.

A Haights Cross Communications Company

http://www.chelseahouse.com

First Printing

1 3 5 7 9 8 6 4 2

Library of Congress Cataloging-in-Publication Data

Allport, Alan, 1970-
  England / Alan Allport.
    v. cm. — (Modern world nations)
Includes index.
Contents: This sceptr'd . . . isle?—The land—England through time—
The English people—Government—Economy—Living in England today.
  ISBN 0-7910-7209-6
  1. England—Juvenile literature. [1. England.] I. Title. II. Series.
DA27.5 .A76 2002
942—dc21

                                                            2002007327

Table of Contents

MODERN WORLD NATIONS

England

Although the small nation of England is separated from Europe by the English Channel, it has still played an enormous role in the history of Europe and the entire world. The English Channel is seen here in a photograph taken from space.

1

This Sceptr'd ... Isle?

I n William Shakespeare's play "Richard II," the King's dying councilman John of Gaunt delivers a fiery patriotic speech that has become one of the classic statements of English national pride:

> This royal throne of kings, this sceptr'd isle . . .
> This precious stone set in the silver sea,
> Which serves it in the office of a wall,
> Or as a moat defensive to a house,
> Against the envy of less happier lands,
> This blessed plot, this earth, this realm, this England.

These are inspiring words, as centuries of Englishmen have attested; but John of Gaunt's passionate speech includes one puzzling but rarely mentioned mistake—England is not an island! Shakespeare did make occasional geographical blunders in his plays, partly out of ignorance—he once suggested that Bohemia in the modern-day Czech Republic has deserts and coastlines, when it has neither—but it is safe to assume that the Bard of Avon was familiar with his own country's physical features. Why then did he let slip what seems like such an obvious blunder?

What Shakespeare was doing, through the words of John of Gaunt, was confusing "England"—a single kingdom bordering Scotland and Wales—with "Great Britain," an island containing all three countries. We should probably not be too hard on the playwright. For hundreds of years people inside and outside of England have been making this same basic error of definition. The details of English life do not help matters much. People speak of the Queen of England—but also the British government; the British Army—but equally the Church of England; and the English language—spoken within the former British Empire. The British fly the Union Jack, but this is not the national flag of England, which is the Cross of St. George (a part of the Union Jack). To confuse things further, the Republic of Ireland is within the British Isles but is most definitely not part of Great Britain or the United Kingdom—as any Irish citizen will gladly inform you. And good luck to anyone traveling to Glasgow or Cardiff who dares to call the locals "English"!

Any book introducing England, then, should begin with an explanation of its terminology. *The British Isles* is a geographical, not a political unit. It is the collective name for the islands in the northwest corner of Europe, bounded on one side by the Atlantic Ocean and the other by the North Sea. There are two principal islands, Great Britain and Ireland, and a host of much smaller ones such as the Isle of Man, the Isle of Wight, the Scottish Hebrides, and the tiny archipelagos of the Orkneys and the Shetlands. *Great Britain* is the largest of the British Isles and it contains three

Great Britain and Ireland are the two principle islands that make up the British Isles. England forms the southern and largest portion of Great Britain, with Wales to its west and Scotland to its north.

countries, England, Scotland, and Wales, each of which was once independent, but is now combined within a single state. The people of Great Britain are often called collectively "the British." Along with the northern part of Ireland, sometimes known as Ulster, these countries make up the *United Kingdom*, or UK for short. To think of a North American analogy, England is to the UK what Pennsylvania or California is to the United States.

This analogy is not quite correct, however, because England is by far the largest, most populous and richest of the four members of the United Kingdom. Historically this has meant that England has tended to dominate the British Isles, sometimes by diplomatic and economic means and sometimes by bloodier military methods. England's relationship with its neighbors has not always been a happy or a proud one, and there are echoes of this today in the religious and ethnic conflict in Northern Ireland. However, it a relationship that is open to continuous change, and one of the more profound developments of recent years has been an increase in the local autonomy of the non-English regions of the UK, for example through the new Scottish Parliament in Edinburgh and Northern Ireland's fledgling government. The increasing decentralization of the United Kingdom creates questions about England's identity and future, something that is discussed in the conclusion to this book.

The proliferation of English words, place-names and associations across the world from New Zealand to Alaska indicates the huge influence that this relatively small country has had in international affairs. Both the United States and Canada were originally founded as English colonies, and millions of modern-day Americans can trace their ancestry back to English emigrants who left the mother country for a new life sometime during the last four hundred years. England has an unusually long tradition of unbroken social institutions such as its royal family and parliament, and the country's rich legacy of kings, castles, pomp and circumstance makes it one of the world's most popular tourist destinations. History aside, England is also a major economic center and its capital, London, is one of the hubs of the global financial marketplace; it also continues to wield important political and diplomatic power. At the beginning of the 20th century, England was at the heart of the largest empire in the history of the world. Although that empire has long vanished, England will have an important role to play in the affairs of the 21st century, although precisely what role that will be is not so clear.

England's longest river, the Thames, runs through the capital city of London. Since water was so important for both transportation and power during the early years of the Industrial Revolution, the Thames has been an important center of industry and settlement for over two centuries.

2

The Land

E ngland is only a part of the United Kingdom, but it is geographically the major part, taking up about 50,000 of the UK's roughly 93,000 square miles in area. This means that England is approximately the size of New York state. England forms the southern, and largest, portion of the island of Great Britain, with Wales to its west and Scotland to its north. Although Great Britain is often thought of as being a very small place, it is actually the eighth largest island in the world, and stretches 600 miles from its northern to its southern extremities.

The British Isles as a whole lie at the northwestern corner of the European mainland, surrounded by several bodies of water. To the southeast is the English Channel, which divides England from France; at its narrowest point, between Dover and Calais, the two countries are a mere 21 miles apart. Eastern Britain is separated from

Scandinavia, the Low Countries, and Germany by the North Sea, a shallow and stormy arm of the Atlantic Ocean. One area of the North Sea, the rich fishing zone known as the Dogger Bank, is barely 50 feet deep in places. Western Ireland and the north and southwest coasts of Great Britain lie directly on the Atlantic Ocean shoreline. Ireland and Britain themselves are divided by the Irish Sea, which lets out into the Atlantic at two conduits, the narrow North Channel strait and the broader St. George's Channel.

All these seas and waterways have had an important influence on the development of English history. Although England has no great river systems, its coast is pockmarked with dozens of bays and inlets that make excellent natural harbors. The convoluted path of the coastline means that no part of the country is more than 75 miles from tidal water. And Great Britain's position astride the shipping lanes of northern Europe gives it an important strategic significance. All these factors have encouraged English settlers throughout the ages to look to the seas for their economic and military strength.

Geology

England's coastline was one of the last to stabilize in Europe, parts of it only reaching their present-day form around 5000 B.C. Before then, the island of Great Britain was still physically connected to the European mainland by a land corridor across what would become the Channel, and much of what we now know as the North Sea was above sea level. These very recent changes—"recent" in the geological sense, anyway—have helped to give England a complex and multi-layered mineral structure. Broadly speaking, the further west and north one goes the older the rock becomes. Ancient, dense igneous (volcanic) formations on the upland plateaus of Cornwall and Cumbria complement much newer alluvial deposits in the flat East Anglian basin. Sandstone, limestone, slate, and chalk banks criss-cross the country, sometimes folded

Great Britain is located at the northwestern corner of the European mainland. England has many natural bays and harbors, and is positioned astride the major shipping lanes of northern Europe.

into small hill chains. The rich coal seams of Kent, Nottingham, and Tyneside, which have proven so important in England's economic development, are formed from plant remains that built up in prehistoric times when much of the country was a moist, humid swamp. England's fossil, rock, and soil record is so intriguing that it is hardly surprising to discover that the modern science of geology was founded by an Englishman, William Smith, who published his national geological survey in 1815—the first such systematic study in the world.

Climate

England is located between about 50 and 55 degrees north, on the same latitude as most of Ontario and Quebec. Its longitude is around 0–1 degrees west; the Greenwich Meridian, which divides the world into the eastern and western hemispheres, is measured from the Royal Observatory in the London suburb of Greenwich. In other circumstances, England's latitudinal position would have given the country a rather forbidding climate, with bitter winters and lots of snow. However, the British Isles are blessed by a weather phenomenon known as the Gulf Stream: warm Caribbean water is channeled along the North American coastline, then swings eastwards across the Atlantic to form the North Atlantic current. This makes the local sea temperature around Great Britain and Ireland considerably higher than it would otherwise register. One of the biggest long-term concerns the British have about changes in global weather patterns caused by environmental damage is that the Gulf Stream may one day close down, causing a precipitous drop in the temperatures around the British Isles.

Because of the Gulf Stream England has a temperate climate, neither unduly hot in summer nor cold in winter. Temperatures typically reach about 70 to 80 degrees Fahrenheit in July and August, then dip to just above freezing in January. There is generally some snow in the winter months, but rarely of blizzard proportions. Other than flooding and coastal erosion, which as we will see below is a serious ecological dilemma, England has no other weather extremes. It does not experience earthquakes, tornadoes, hurricanes, or severe heat waves. It is perhaps ironic then that this mild and unassuming climate should have gotten such a terrible reputation! The Roman writer Tacitus was the first foreigner to describe England's weather as "objectionable," and ever since then it has become a standing joke that the country has the worst weather in the world. The problem is that the same Gulf Stream currents that bring such vital warm water also propel cloud banks along with them. These clouds, which have picked up plenty of Atlantic Ocean moisture along the way, break across the western British Isles and regularly douse much of Britain and Ireland in rain showers. Over 60 inches of rain will fall on average in the worst-affected English region—the northwestern Lake District. England's green and pleasant land owes its existence to regular precipitation, but that is small comfort to the local population which must endure what can seem like endless, dreary dousing. The clouds also obscure much of the natural sunlight, making England a frequently gray, overcast country. The fickleness of the weather has turned it into one of the major preoccupations of conversation, and the nation's TV viewers are riveted by the updates from the meteorological office every day.

Southern England

For convenience, England can be divided into four geographical zones. The first is southern England, from the tip of Land's End at the farthest western point of Cornwall to the port of Dover in Kent. Traditionally, the lush lowlands of southern England have provided the best of Great Britain's farming zones, and before the onset of northern industrialization in the 19th century, most population growth was concentrated here—as it once again is with the recent decline in heavy industry. The Thames, which flows eastward 210 miles from its source in the

Chiltern Hills to its sea outlet at the Nore estuary, is England's longest river. The southeastern valley of the Thames has long been a center of human settlement, with the sprawling metropolitan area of Greater London now at its hub. Immediately surrounding London are the so-called "Home Counties" which include Buckinghamshire, Kent, Essex, and Surrey. These once distinct regions are becoming steadily swallowed up by the capital's growth, but are popular with London workers who commute from their homes by train every day. Further south are the Channel ports, such as Portsmouth, Southampton, and Folkestone. Brighton, also on the coast, has been a popular vacation spot for centuries. Southeastern England is mostly flat, but there are two modest parallel uplands, the North and South Downs.

Southwestern England is much more rugged and forbidding. The "West Country," as it is known, remained a lawless area until the early 18th century, and was the haunt of smugglers and coastal "wreckers" who attempted to coax passing ships onto the rocks to seize their cargoes. Legends continue to surround the many prehistoric stone circles and monuments that decorate the area, and the wizard Merlin's magical cave was reputed to be found here. Dartmoor and Exmoor are the region's two characteristic national parks, bleak expanses of woodland and heather with a desolate beauty. Further north the county of Gloucestershire, which straddles the Severn estuary, contains the port of Bristol-upon-Avon. Bristol has been an important trading and maritime center since the Middle Ages, and was the starting point for John Cabot's first expedition to North America in 1497. The river Avon, which forms one of the tributaries of the Severn, flows through the charming Cotswolds, a ridge of picturesque limestone hills.

The Midlands and East Anglia

Central England is made up of the East and West Midlands and the flat but fertile fenlands of East Anglia. The Midlands are Shakespeare country, focused particularly on the immortal Bard's birthplace of Stratford, which is also the modern-day home of the Royal Shakespeare theater company. They are also heavily industrialized, containing England's second largest city, Birmingham, and some equally built-up urban conurbations like Wolverhampton, Coventry, and Nottingham. Much of the West Midlands region is known as the "Black Country" because of the thick coatings of grime and coal dust that became familiar to its residents during the Industrial Revolution. Although the Midlands acquired a lot of its wealth from the production of heavy manufacturing goods and the automobile industry, it is also famous for fine pottery and ceramics.

East Anglia's dense marshes kept that region effectively cut off from the rest of England for many centuries, and even now its population density is unusually low. These fenlands have now mostly been drained, but the region continues to resemble the flat polder country of Holland more than it does other parts of the UK. The market town of Norwich and the great university city of Cambridge are among the more important urban centers. East Anglia's farming land is especially rich and provides much of Britain's cereal and potato crop needs.

Yorkshire and the North West

As we progress further northwards the country begins to be divided by a great hill chain called the Pennines—sometimes known as the "backbone of England"—which rises in the Peak District and continues northward towards the Scottish border. Lying roughly on either side of the Pennines are the historic rival counties of Lancashire in the west and Yorkshire in the east. Lancashire traditionally boasted two enormous industrial regions, the great manufacturing hub of Manchester and the Atlantic port of Liverpool. But each of these cities has now been given a special administrative status of its own. Yorkshire, too, has several important industrial cities, such as Leeds, Hull, and Sheffield. All of these 19th century behemoths have suffered enormously due to the decline of heavy industry in the last hundred years, and the Pennine counties—perhaps England's nearest equivalent to the U.S. "rust-belt"—have suffered relative depopulation. However, economic woes have not dispelled any of Yorkshire or Lancashire's local civic pride, which includes the use of incomprehensible regional accents and a "straight-talking" attitude towards life that is contrasted unfavorably with that of the more effete South. This region is one of the best examples of the stark contrast between England's rural beauty and its grittier industrial legacy. Handsome river valleys and moorlands contrast with disused factory chimneys and textile mills. The West Yorkshire Moors, famous for their association with the novels of the Brontë sisters Emily and Charlotte, are right next door to the former cotton metropolis of Bradford.

Northern England

Everyone in England recognizes a difference in character between the north and the south of the country, but there is much dispute about where the boundary between the two lies; no "Mason-Dixon line" exists to clarify the issue. An old joke says that the north begins outside of Watford, just a few miles from Greater London! A more realistic line of division would be from the Mersey to the Humber river estuaries, on the southern fringes of Lancashire and Yorkshire. For our current purposes, however, northern England will be taken to mean the region nearest to Scotland, especially the large counties of Northumberland, Durham, and Cumbria. This is historically disputed land, which throughout the centuries often changed hands with the Scots and was the scene of bitter battles and sieges. Its military importance is reflected in the large number of surviving medieval castles, such as Alnwick, and the great Roman fortification of Hadrian's Wall. Cumbria is home to the Lake District, a region of hilly moorlands and deep freshwater lakes that is arguably England's most picturesque region and its archetypal "beauty spot." The Lakes contain England's

Cumbria, home of England's Lake District, is one of the most scenic areas in the country, and is well known for its sheep farming. Despite the region's beauty, however, the farming industry has been negatively affected by outbreaks of foot and mouth disease among the sheep in recent years.

highest point, Scafell Pike, which is only 3,210 feet above sea level and easily manageable by hill-walkers. It also boasts the country's principal body of freshwater, 10.5 mile-long Lake Windermere. While less spectacular, Northumberland also contains some ruggedly attractive scenery such as the Cheviot

Hills. The Tyne and Tees river estuaries form a large industrial area that includes Newcastle and Middlesborough, once major shipbuilding and iron-working concerns, but now fallen on harder times.

Environmental Concerns

Because of the rapid pace of their country's industrialization, the English were among the first people in the world to become seriously concerned about the effects of pollution on their natural environment. This is not to say that the problem of pollution was tackled quickly. As late as the 1950s, cities like London were grimy and blackened, with terrible public health records. The famous London fogs of Sherlock Holmes legend were actually formed by belching chimney smoke, and were responsible for the premature deaths of thousands of people from respiratory-related illnesses. But the pioneering 1956 Clean Air Act forced industrial manufacturers to implement more effective pollution controls, and this made England's towns and cities much more pleasant places in which to work and reside. The replacement of household fireplaces with gas and electric heating also helped to sweeten the urban air. Ironically, the collapse of England's industrial base also shut off its factory smokestacks and thus contributed to an overall improvement in air quality, as well as a reduction in the number of toxicants in the water supply. England at the turn of the 21st century is a much healthier place to live than it was one hundred years ago, although there are still major international controversies over the acid rain produced by the country's coal-burning electric power stations and the contamination of seawater by radioactive waste from nuclear reactors.

If the more pessimistic projections about rising world sea levels caused by the "greenhouse effect" are accurate, then England's greatest ecological threat in the new century may come from persistent flooding of low-lying land. Because no part of England is more than 75 miles from tidal waters, as was mentioned earlier, this means that few areas of the country are completely safe from the effects of higher sea levels. Already the winter inundation of parts of southwestern and northern England close to major rivers has become a dreaded almost-annual event, and the government is under pressure to construct sophisticated defenses like London's Thames tidal barrage in other vulnerable regions. The erosion of shoreline cliffs has combined with this problem; as the softer rocks of the coast are steadily worn away, the flat and unprotected land behind them becomes open to the sea and may even be permanently covered by salt-water. England's coastal outline, which was thought to have stabilized seven thousand years ago, may be on the move again. It is partly for this reason that "Green" issues have come to the forefront of many British people's minds, as indicated by the rise to prominence of important environmental pressure groups like Greenpeace and Friends of the Earth.

England is home to one of the most mysterious landmarks in the world:
Stonehenge. This grouping of gigantic stones dates to prehistoric times,
and historians are still not entirely sure what its purpose was.

England Through Time

E ngland, its people boast, has not been successfully invaded by a foreign country since 1066. This is a bit misleading, because several English kings were overthrown by "pretenders" to the throne supported by armies from abroad—both Edward II (1284–1327) and James II (1633–1701) were removed from power in this way, for example. But it is true that England is one of the oldest continually existing states in the world, with an unbroken line of succession dating back well over a thousand years. From the Spanish Armada in 1588 to Napoleon Bonaparte's fleet in 1805 to Nazi Germany's Air Force in 1940, the English have beaten back successive waves of would-be invaders from mainland Europe. This has encouraged the English to think of themselves as a people apart, living aloof from the rest of the continent in "splendid isolation," and developing their own unique customs and traditions.

No country is really all that isolated, however, and in fact England has been in continuous interaction with the rest of the British Isles, mainland Europe, and the world since its earliest times. Modern England owes its language, its religions, its legal and political institutions, and the diversity of its population to influences from abroad. No country that has had so many foreign empires—in medieval France, in Ireland, in North America, and eventually in Africa, Asia, and India—can expect to be unchanged as a result.

Prehistoric England

As we saw in Chapter 2, up to seven thousand years ago Great Britain was still physically connected to the rest of Europe by a land bridge. This allowed wandering tribes of hunter-gatherers to cross from France into southern England, and over the centuries they slowly expanded across the rest of the British peninsula. No-one knows for sure when the first human beings arrived in Britain, but the oldest remains ever discovered are 500,000 years old and date from the "Paleolithic," or Old Stone Age, period. During the last Ice Age, which ended around 11,000 B.C., much of northern Britain was covered by frozen glaciers and forbidding Arctic tundra. The gradual retreat of the ice brought a warming of the land and coastal waters, encouraging thick forests rich in wildlife to emerge, and also raising the sea level to swallow up the land bridge. The higher temperatures made England more habitable, but also cut it off from developments in the rest of Europe. For this reason, new technologies like farming (4000 B.C.), bronze (2000 B.C.), and iron (600–500 B.C.) were relatively slow to arrive in England.

The first identifiable English civilization is known as "Windmill Hill" after the archeological site in Wiltshire where it was discovered. Windmill Hill society, which developed around six thousand years ago, was based on agriculture and animal husbandry; its people used flint tools and had complex religious rites and burial customs. About 2000 B.C., Windmill Hill culture was supplanted by the so-called "Beaker" people who emigrated from what is now the Netherlands and northern Germany. In addition to more advanced metal-working skills and trading patterns— Beaker goods have been found as far away as the eastern Mediterranean—they constructed elaborate monuments and stone circles, by far the most famous of which is Stonehenge on Salisbury Plain, also in Wiltshire. Stonehenge had apparently long been an important ritual site, but the Beaker people erected the massive stone slabs that we see there today. Some of these mighty monoliths weigh 50 tons and were specially brought from Wales, over 200 miles away. No one is really sure what the purpose of Stonehenge was, though because of its peculiar alignment to the stars it has been suggested that it may have been a sort of calendar.

Between 700 and 300 B.C. small groups of migrants from mainland Europe brought Celtic culture to England. The Celts had knowledge of iron working, and made beautifully decorated weapons and armor. They exploited the tin mines of Cornwall for the first time, trading tin for Italian silver that their chieftains jealously guarded in newly constructed hill forts. For all their technological achievements, however, the Celts would prove no match for the invaders from the south who were to change English history forever.

Roman England

In 55 B.C. the Roman general and statesman Julius Caesar, who was campaigning in Gaul (modern France), made a tentative raid on Kent. He and his troops soon left for other adventures, but the Romans did not forget about this dark corner of the known world that they referred to as

"Britannia." Almost a hundred years later Caesar's successor, Emperor Claudius, decided to return—and this time, for good. In 43 A.D. he sent four Legions of elite Roman infantry across the Channel, and in a lightning campaign subdued all of the native Celtic tribes of southeastern England. In follow-up expeditions the Romans conquered the rest of England and Wales, and established a frontier along the modern border with Scotland. For the next four hundred years England would be part of the classical civilization of the Mediterranean.

Roman dominance did not go unchallenged. In 60 A.D. a Celtic queen, Boudicca, from what is now East Anglia, led a rebellion against the cruel policies of the Roman governor, and her tribal warriors sacked several forts and towns (including London, then a small settlement) until they were defeated at the hands of the Legions. Boudicca committed suicide, but her proud stand against tyranny later became a symbol of English nationhood. One of the stranger details of her story is that she is believed to be buried under one of the platforms of King's Cross railroad station in London. The Romans also suffered persistent raiding from the native tribes in Scotland. Rather than conquer such a thinly populated country, the Emperor Hadrian ordered the construction of a huge defensive wall across Britannia's northern border, from the Solway Firth to Tyneside. Hadrian's Wall, much of which stands to this day, is a triumph of Roman engineering.

During the centuries of Roman occupation, settlers moved from elsewhere in the Empire and built sophisticated towns, roads, and fortifications. Spectacular examples of Roman artistry can still be seen in places like the spa-town of Bath, where the colonists used the local hot mineral springs to construct an elaborate bathhouse dedicated to the goddess Minerva. Many modern English cities such as Manchester, York, Carlisle, and Canterbury were founded as Roman military or civilian settlements. Towards the end of Roman rule, Christianity also came to England for the first time.

The Dark Ages

In 410 A.D. the Emperor Honorius, beleaguered by barbarian invasions elsewhere, sent a proclamation to the Romans in Britannia informing them that the imperial army could no longer defend them and that they would henceforth have to look after themselves. With this abdication of responsibility, the Roman presence in England effectively ended. Not that there was any longer a distinctive "Roman" community there anyway. By the 5th century A.D. the colonists had intermarried with the local Celtic peoples and become largely indistinguishable from one another. But the departure of the Roman Legions left England dangerously unprotected against foreign invaders.

The period between the 5th and 11th centuries is sometimes called "The Dark Ages" because so little written evidence remains from it. We know that England was attacked in the 400s by successive waves of pagan tribes from northwest Europe—Frisians, Jutes, Angles, and Saxons. These invaders, collectively known as the "Anglo-Saxons," pushed much of the original Romano-British population out of England; its remnants retreated to Cornwall, Wales, and even as far as Brittany on the French coast. After they had exhausted their appetite for looting and pillaging, the Anglo-Saxons began to settle England permanently. The country lost its political unity and was subdivided into many rival kingdoms, the most important of which were Wessex in the southwest, Mercia in the Midlands, and Northumbria in the north. During the 7th century A.D. the Anglo-Saxons were converted to Christianity by missionaries from Ireland and Rome.

In the 9th and 10th centuries a new breed of barbarian

invaders appeared; these were the Vikings, or Norsemen, of Scandinavia. For decades the Viking raiders caused terror and destruction throughout England, but eventually, like the Anglo-Saxons before them, they chose to establish a permanent presence. This was short-lived, however, because the kingdom of Wessex was on the rise. In 927 one of its rulers, Athelstan, retook the Viking territories and became the first Anglo-Saxon monarch of a reunited England. After Athelstan's reign, England was never again a politically divided country.

The Norman Conquest and the Middle Ages

In 1066, one of Athelstan's descendents, St. Edward the Confessor (1003–1066), an exceptionally pious king who built the original Westminster Abbey, died without an heir. The Earl of Wessex, Harold (1020–1066), claimed the English throne. Edward's French cousin William of Normandy (1028–1087) also sought this rich prize, however, and so promptly invaded England. Their armies met at Hastings in Sussex on October 14, and after a fierce battle Harold was killed. The victor, now William the Conqueror, marched in triumph to London and so began the Norman Kingdom of England.

William and the Anglo-French kings who followed him left a powerful impression on English history. The Norman aristocracy imposed the 'feudal' system throughout England, in which society was divided into social classes—peasantry, knights, barons, and the king at the top. Each paid homage to their superiors by service or payment. William ordered the construction of castles across his kingdom, and made a tax survey of the whole country that was compiled as the "Domesday Book." Much of the shire county system of regional English government dates from the Norman period.

The Norman kings of England were eventually replaced

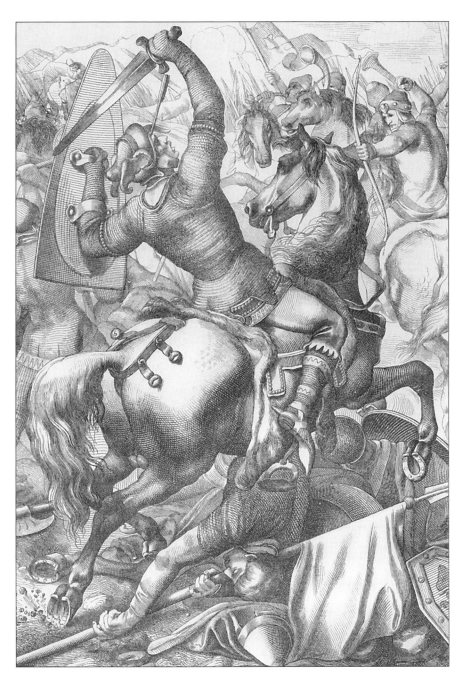

In October 1066, William, Duke of Normandy, defeated King Harold II of England at the Battle of Hastings. William soon became known as "William the Conqueror," and he took control of the English throne as the first Norman king.

by another related dynasty, the Plantagenets. Thanks to their Norman inheritance, the Plantagenet monarchs remained powerful landholders in France, and throughout the Middle Ages many kings and queens of England spent more time in France than they did in their 'homeland' (and spoke better French than English, too). Edward III (1312–1377) even claimed the French throne for himself, and so set off the "Hundred Years' War" between the two countries. Despite impressive English victories at battles like Crecy (1346) and Agincourt (1415), the French eventually rallied and fought off the Plantagenet threat. By the mid 1400s most of the English possessions in France had been lost forever, and England's kings were in any case preoccupied with domestic conflict back across the Channel.

The War of the Roses and the Reformation

Edward III's successors were divided between the dynasties, or "houses," of York and Lancaster. The struggle between the two houses, which came to dominate the 15th century, was known as the War of the Roses because of the Yorkist and Lancastrian symbols—a white rose and a red rose, respectively. The war seemed to end in 1483 with the coronation of Richard III (1452–1485), a powerful Yorkist king. But rumors that Richard had murdered his two young nephews, one of whom was the deposed King Edward V, destabilized his regime and he was killed two years later at the Battle of Bosworth Field by Henry VII (1457–1509) of the Welsh Tudor dynasty.

Henry VII's reign brought much-needed stability to the country, but his successor Henry VIII (1491–1547) created new strife, this time religious. Henry's marriage to Catherine of Aragon had produced no male heir, and so he wished to divorce her and marry a younger woman, Anne Boleyn. This required the permission of the Pope, who was at the time busy trying to suppress Martin Luther's Protestant heresy in

Germany and so dared not alienate Catherine's nephew, the Holy Roman Emperor Charles V. Henry grew exasperated by Papal stalling, and finally in 1533 ordered Parliament to pass an "Act of Supremacy" making the King the head of the new Church of England, which would henceforth be totally independent of Catholic Rome. Almost by accident, England had become a Protestant country.

Henry went through six wives in the end, and the children of his various marriages had very different ideas about the new Church. Edward VI (1537–1553) was a staunch Protestant, but reigned too briefly to have much influence. His sister, "Bloody" Mary I (1516–1558), was an equally rigid Catholic; during her five years on the throne, she persecuted English Protestants and made herself a figure of popular hatred. The sister who replaced her, Elizabeth I (1533–1603) was a compromiser. Although she kept England independent of Rome and angered extremists of both sides, Elizabeth sought—and achieved—an important measure of religious stability.

The Birth of Britain

Few people would have guessed at her coronation that the young and inexperienced Elizabeth would become "Good Queen Bess," the ruler of England for over forty years and one of the nation's greatest monarchs. Her finest hour was in 1588 when Philip II of Spain, Mary I's widower who was fanatically determined to return England to Catholicism, launched a huge fleet in an attempt to invade England and reassert Papal authority. Philip's Armada was defeated by Elizabeth's warships and bad weather, and the victory signaled England's beginnings as a great naval power.

Elizabeth died a childless and unmarried "Virgin Queen." Her successor as King of England was James I (1566–1625) of the House of Stuart, who already ruled Scotland as James VI. This royal union between the two countries, which had traditionally been at loggerheads, was a watershed in the history of the British Isles. Wales had already united with England in 1283, and now James, who called himself the first "King of Great Britain," was the undisputed ruler of the whole island. Unification, however, was far from complete. England and Scotland still maintained separate parliaments until 1707, when the Act of Union formally merged the two countries into a single state—the United Kingdom—administered from London. A similar Act of Union with Ireland would follow in 1801. In theory at least, there were no more English, Scottish, Welsh or Irish people—there were only "Britons."

Civil Wars and Revolutions

Before this national unification was complete, however, the English had to undergo three traumatic revolutions against the authority of their kings. James' son, Charles I (1600–1649) was an autocratic monarch who sought to rule England without the assistance of Parliament. This provoked so much hostility that fighting broke out between factions of the country loyal to the Crown and those who supported the liberties of Parliament. The Civil War of the 1640s ended with Charles under arrest; he was publicly executed in 1649 as a traitor. This stunning decision was followed by the creation of an eleven-year 'Protectorate' under the Parliamentarian general Oliver Cromwell. In reality the protectorate was really a Republic, the only such government in English history.

By the time of Cromwell's death in 1658, the Protectorate had become extremely unpopular, and the English people welcomed the return of the dead king's son Charles II (1630–1685) to the throne. But Charles showed worrying signs of sympathy for Catholicism, and his successor James II (1633–1701) was an openly avowed Catholic. This was too much for the Protestant English Parliament, and it secretly

After decades of fighting between those who wanted a king and those who wanted a parliamentary form of government, the English people invited William of Orange from the Netherlands to take the throne of England in 1688. William was crowned King William III, and his wife became Mary II. This bloodless transfer of power is often referred to as the Glorious Revolution.

invited James' son-in-law, the Dutchman William of Orange (1650–1702) to seize power in a military coup. William landed in England in 1688, and in the so-called Glorious Revolution deposed James, who fled into exile in France. William was confirmed as the new monarch, although on the firm understanding that henceforth Parliament would make most day-to-day political decisions.

The American War of Independence can also be seen as the third in this series of insurrections against English royal authority. England's first colony in North America was founded in Virginia in 1607 during James I's reign, and in the century that followed a string of English settlements grew up on the eastern seaboard, from Georgia to Newfoundland. France's defeat in the 'French and Indian War' of 1756–1763 guaranteed the colonists' safety from foreign invasion, but it also made them less tolerant of London's sometimes high-handed governance. In 1775 the colonists, following the tradition established by Parliament in the 1640s and 1680s, revolted against their "tyrant" king, George III (1738–1820). The war, never popular in Britain, ended with the formation of the United States of America and the creation of a second English-speaking Atlantic power.

The Industrial Revolution

While political revolt was taking place in America in the late 1700s, a less bloody but just as important economic upheaval was happening in England at the same time—the phenomenon known as the Industrial Revolution. This was the introduction of new factory methods and energy sources such as wind, water, coal, and steam to create a massive increase in economic production. Starting with textiles and moving on to iron and eventually steel-making, England became by the early 19th century the industrial powerhouse of the world. The effects of these new technologies were immense. Enormous northern cities like Manchester, Liverpool, Leeds, and Sheffield, dominated by smoke-belching factories, grew up within a single generation. Railroads, invented in England, connected the country together for the first time. Middle-class businessmen grew rich on factory profits and demanded representation in

Parliament; working-class trade unionists also insisted on more political power, as well as social legislation to restrict bad working conditions and improve appalling slum housing. The Industrial Revolution changed the shape of England itself. By the dawn of the 20th century the "green and pleasant land" imagined by William Blake had become a wealthy and powerful, but in many places dirty and unhealthy.

Pax Britannica

In 1805 the Royal Navy under Admiral Lord Nelson decisively defeated the French and Spanish fleets at the Battle of Trafalgar. For the next hundred years, no other power dared challenge the United Kingdom's naval might. The result was that Britain, aided by its wealth from the Industrial Revolution, was able to carve up much of the world in a huge colonial empire. During the 64-year reign of Queen Victoria (1819–1901), the British Empire spread from Canada to Australia and New Zealand; from Singapore and Hong Kong to Nigeria and South Africa; and above all, across India—the jewel in the imperial crown. By Queen Victoria's death about one quarter of the land surface of the Earth was controlled from London. The 19th century is sometimes called the era of the "Pax Britannica," the peace of Britain, because the world was so dominated by one superpower that no major wars could break out. This is a bit misleading, because the British had to fight quite a lot of short, sharp battles against indigenous peoples from Zululand to China who were not always keen at being part of this new empire. But the overwhelming technological advantage that Europeans enjoyed over non-Europeans usually ended the fighting quickly enough. As the English writer Hilaire Belloc put it, with bitter irony:

> Whatever happens, we have got
> The Maxim gun [a type of machine gun]—and they
>   have not.

England and the End of Empire

Although by 1914 Britain's imperial might looked all-powerful, in fact the United Kingdom was steadily losing ground to industrial rivals like Germany and the United States. The outbreak of World War I that year signaled the beginning of Britain's long decline. During the war's four terrible years, the British Empire lost a million men and the country was left with crippling financial debts. During the war a rebellion broke out in Dublin, Ireland, and though it was quickly quashed the political mood in Ireland afterwards was so hostile that in 1921 the British government agreed to allow the southern part of the country to leave the United Kingdom. During the 1920s and 1930s Britain's worldwide commitments actually grew larger, but it now had much less money with which to deal with them. The rise of dictatorships in Germany, Italy, and Japan meant new danger. In 1939, Nazi Germany attacked Poland, and Britain and France declared war on Hitler's Third Reich. The following year the Germans conquered France in a startling six-week victory and brought England to the brink of invasion. Only the heroism of the Royal Air Force pilots in the "Battle of Britain" and the fortitude of Britain's wartime prime minister, Sir Winston Churchill, prevented complete defeat at the hands of the Nazis.

In due course the Soviet Union and the United States entered the war, and by 1945 the Axis powers had been defeated. But the United Kingdom was now virtually bankrupt and unable to maintain its worldwide empire. Two years after the war's end India became independent, and throughout the following two decades the rest of the former British Empire peacefully seceded. By the 1960s Britain had recovered somewhat from the worst effects of the war, and living conditions for ordinary people have continued to improve, thanks in part to the extensive post-war welfare state. It is clear, though, that the days of imperial glory are now gone forever. In an odd return to its roots, England is becoming once again a small kingdom off the northwest coast of Europe like that which Athelstan ruled a thousand years ago.

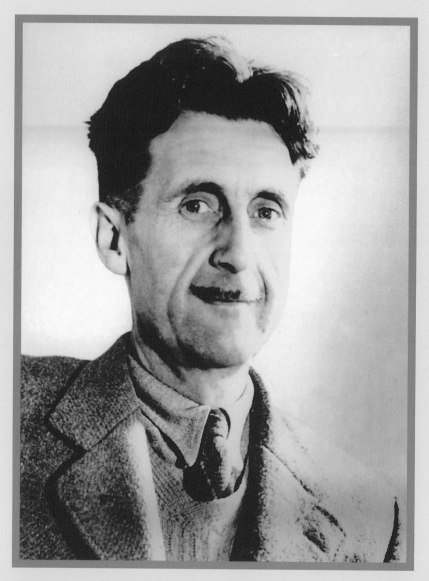

English writer George Orwell (1903–1950) said that England was very different from other European countries. The many changes in government, geographic territory, and culture that have taken place throughout England's long history have had many effects on the nation and have made it the interesting place it is today.

4

The English People

Author and journalist George Orwell once wrote "When you come back to England from any foreign country, you have immediately the sensation of breathing a different air. The crowds in the big towns, with their mild knobby faces, their bad teeth and gentle manners, are different from a European crowd." Orwell's point about the uniqueness of England and its people is something that many observers have remarked upon over the centuries. It is strange perhaps that a country that technically speaking has not existed for almost 300 years (since the Act of Union between England and Scotland in 1707, which transformed them both into Great Britain) still retains such obvious distinctive qualities. But the English have not remained unchanged. The influence of 19th century industrialization and its eventual decline, war, the weakening of old class and religious ties, emigration to the British Empire and immigration from it, have all had a profound influence on English life and manners. But there remains a lingering sense of England's continuity through time. As Orwell put it: "It is somehow bound up with solid breakfasts and gloomy Sundays, smoky towns and winding roads, green fields and red pillar boxes. It stretches into the future and the past, there is something in it that persists, as in a living creature."

Settlement Patterns and Early Immigration.

Humans have lived in England for at least half a million years. Throughout its early history settlers traveled from many directions—westwards across the North Sea from Germany and Scandinavia, northwards from what is now France, southwards from Scotland, even eastwards from Ireland. It is not always clear whether the new cultures that successively appeared in England up until 1066—Windmill Hill, Beaker, Celtic, Roman, Anglo-Saxon, Viking, Norman—always involved a physical change in population, or simply represent the influence of new ideas and languages. In most cases it was probably a combination of both. Invasions from abroad often meant the dispersal of old communities and the arrival of foreign immigrants, but many local inhabitants may have assimilated into the arriving culture and "become," say, Roman or Viking. The modern science of genetics, which uses DNA evidence to trace ancestry, has made some interesting discoveries related to this theory. In 1997, for example, scientists proved that a schoolteacher living in the town of Cheddar in southwest England was directly related to a 9,000-year-old man whose skeleton was discovered just half a mile away from his descendant's home!

After the Norman conquest in the 11th century there were fewer mass influxes of new people to England. However, smaller groups of immigrants continued to arrive, such as German merchants, Dutch textile workers, and French Protestant (or "Huguenot") refugees from the staunchly

Catholic kingdom of Louis XIV. Before the mid-1700s, the population remained relatively small by European standards, at around five million people. These were mostly concentrated in small farming communities in southern England. London was the country's only really large city.

All this changed about 250 years ago with the introduction of more efficient agricultural techniques and the beginning of the Industrial Revolution. By 1811 England's population had doubled to 10 million, and by the 1860s it had quadrupled; at the turn of the 20th century 35 million people lived in England. This was not only the result of increased birth and lowered death rates, but also of huge emigrations from other parts of the British Isles, especially Ireland, which was ravaged by famine in the mid-19th century (today about 800,000 people in England can trace their ancestry to Ireland). The increase is even more surprising when you consider that millions of English men and women were leaving the country at the same time to settle in North America and other parts of the British Empire. The distribution of population altered drastically, as enormous industrial cities sprang up in northern and central England. Most people abandoned the countryside for the towns in search of factory work. During the 20th century some of these changes reversed themselves, reflecting the decline of industrialization. Economic depressions reduced the populations of the big northern cities like Newcastle and Liverpool, and southern England again became the focus of demographic growth. This was especially true of Greater London, which now has a population of about 7.3 million.

However, England continued, and continues, to be an extremely urbanized society. In the 1991 census over 90 percent of the population described themselves as living in a city or a suburban area. The country's population density is also extremely high, at 930 persons per square mile (compared to 600 persons per square mile for the United Kingdom as a whole); within Europe, only the tiny Netherlands is as tightly packed as England. In 1998 the population of the UK was estimated at approximately 59 million people, about 50 million of whom live in England. To put this into American perspective, England is a country about the size of New York state but with the population of New York *and* California combined. These numbers have not increased all that much since the 1960s, reflecting a very significant slowdown in the birth rate from the hectic growth spurts of the 19th century. Like many European countries, England is now barely at replacement level—in other words, there are scarcely enough births to keep the population from falling, excluding the effects of immigration. This also means that the national age distribution is changing rapidly, with more elderly people relative to young. Such a disparity may create economic problems in the future, as a dwindling work force attempts to support an ever-increasing retirement generation.

The "New Commonwealth" British

One of the most significant changes in England's population structure has been the immigration of non-Europeans from the "New Commonwealth" nations of the Caribbean, Africa, and South Asia, all of whom began arriving in large numbers for the first time after World War II. These immigrants were initially encouraged to come to Britain because of a shortfall in the native manpower pool. However, during the 1960s increasing resentment of the new Britons pushed the government to enact much tougher immigration policies. Racial discrimination and ethnically-inspired violence were unfortunately prevalent in many towns with large non-white populations, and this culminated in a series of violent urban riots in the early 1980s. Insensitive and racially-prejudiced policing in some large cities helped to stoke the flames.

Tensions continue to exist in some areas; there have been, for example, serious disturbances in the town of Oldham in Lancashire because of racial fighting between Asian and

In recent decades, England has faced problems of racial discrimination and violence, especially in cities with a high population of new immigrants. These racial tensions are made worse by groups such as these young white supremacists, who are seen giving a Nazi salute during a political march in 1980.

white teenage gangs. A very small but noisy racist political movement called the British National Party (BNP) has made inroads in places like Oldham. And immigration continues to be a controversial issue, partly because of high-profile stories like the large number of Kurdish and Afghan refugees who have recently sought asylum in England, many entering the country illegally. Thankfully, however, race relations have generally improved, and English people of color have adjusted quite successfully to their adopted country's lifestyle. This is partly the result of conscious assimilation, and partly a reflection of the way that England itself has changed because of its New Commonwealth citizens. Just as a black Peer of the Realm now sits in the House of Lords and Indian entertainers have become popular TV celebrities, so curry has become a fixture of England's national cuisine and cities like London are a gorgeous tapestry of people, stores, and goods from all across the former Empire. As of 2000, only about 5 percent of the total UK population was non-white, predominantly from the West Indies, India, Pakistan, Bangladesh, Hong Kong, and sub-Saharan Africa. But this small segment has had a powerful impact on the national culture.

Language

The vast majority of the population speaks English. A tiny number of ancient indigenous tongues like Cornish still linger, and some of the New Commonwealth residents are bilingual in Hindi, Urdu, and other Asian languages, but these are unusual exceptions. The massive international success of English—it is the most widespread language in the world, now used on six continents and second only to Mandarin Chinese in absolute number of speakers—has been both a blessing and a curse to its original speakers. Its universality makes it much easier for English goods and services to travel across global frontiers, and the language's literature and ideas have had an incalculable influence on people everywhere. However, this very ease of use has discouraged English people from learning foreign languages, which can be a disadvantage in dealings with, for example, other members of the European Union. Also, English as spoken in Great Britain, is now only one sub-category of the language—sometimes called "British English" to distinguish it from other sorts—and is not even the most popular variety, given the rise of the influence of the United States. Sometimes the English rather feel that they have had their own language stolen away from them.

The stereotypical, "posh" English accent is actually only spoken by a small number of people, mainly in southern England. Its technical name is Received Pronunciation, although it is sometimes called "BBC English" after the well-known broadcasting company that has encouraged its use, or "the Queen's English" after its most famous speaker. Elsewhere in England people use a dizzying array of regional dialects and accents, many of which are almost incomprehensible to outsiders. Amongst the most famous are Cockney, spoken in London; Scouse, from Liverpool; Geordie, from Newcastle and Tyneside; and Brummie, from the Birmingham area. The biggest overall difference is between northern and southern varieties of English. Northerners tend to use shorter vowel sounds, for example pronouncing the "a" in the word "bath" in the same way as "fat"; southerners would pronounce it like the "a" in "father." In recent years the distinctive branches of southern accent have started to be overtaken by a generic London-based dialect known as "Estuary English," loosely based on Cockney.

In British English, words are frequently spelled or used differently from the American version of the language. Words ending in "or" are generally written as "our," like colour and flavour, for instance. A faucet is "tap," a vacation is a "holiday," and an elevator is a "lift." An American who wants to check under the hood of his station wagon while pumping gas will be out of luck in England, although he can always take a look under the bonnet of his estate car while getting petrol at the garage!

Religion

Unlike the United States, England has an official state religion. The Queen is the supreme head of the Church of England, a Protestant Christian faith also known as "Anglicanism" that is better known in North America as the Episcopal Church. Because of its official nature, the Church of England has some unusual legal rights and responsibilities. The monarch appoints all of its senior clergy, although this task is usually delegated to the prime minister, and at least until the recent reforms of the House of Lords its bishops had permanent seats in Parliament. The Church's leader after the

Queen, the Archbishop of Canterbury, crowns the monarch at his or her coronation and is traditionally seen as being charged with the nation's moral and spiritual well-being. An Act of Parliament is required to make any major changes to the Church's constitution. Despite all this, however, the Anglican Church receives no money from the state, and despite its large landholdings the Church today is suffering from serious financial problems because of the number of ancient and increasingly decrepit places of worship under its care. The collapse in its active membership (for which see below) has only exacerbated its problems. Anglicanism is a moderate form of Protestantism in which priests have a large amount of discretion about how they conduct their services; the main distinction is between "Low" Church practices, which are similar to Methodism, and the "High" Church, which is largely indistinguishable from Catholicism.

Until the mid-19th century, Roman Catholics were ineligible to join many of the important institutions of English life, including Parliament and the Universities of Oxford and Cambridge. They achieved freedom of worship in the Victorian period, although no significant Catholic community existed until the influx of Irish immigrants around the same period. Today English Catholics are fully integrated into national society, and the only trace of the old restrictions is in the choice of monarch; by law, no king or queen of England can be, or marry, a Catholic. Other important Christian sects that began or developed in England include Methodism, Baptism, Quakerism, and Pentecostalism, and these communities still exist today.

According to 1995 figures 43 percent of the UK population is Anglican, nearly 10 percent Catholic, and 10 percent part of another Protestant or Greek Orthodox denomination. Does this mean, then, that Britain is a Christian country? Well, yes and no. Attendance figures at regular Church services of all types have plummeted in recent years. Fewer than two million

The British monarchy has become a ceremonial and fairly modern institution through the twentieth and early twenty-first centuries, but it still has certain traditions, such as the requirement that the monarch be a member of the Church of England. England mourned the loss of the Queen Mother (seen here in a 1985 photograph) who died on March 30, 2002, at the age of 101.

people are regular communicants at Anglican churches, and there are about the same number of practicing Catholics. The UK is a much more secular country than the United States, with nearly a third of the population expressing no particular religious faith at all and even those who are nominally members of a church rarely taking part in its services. No amount of promotion on the part of religious leaders seems to be able to budge this spiritual indifference. On the other hand, most Britons still see traditional Christian values as important and the majority continues to affirm a belief in God, however vaguely this is sometimes expressed. Formal Christianity has declined enormously, as in the rest of Europe, but a lingering sense of the church's ethical ideals remains.

Although their numbers are relatively small, the non-Christian faiths in England are in some ways much more vibrant. Because the UK was a sanctuary from Nazi persecutions during World War II, it now has the second largest Jewish population in Europe. There are about 300,000 Jews living in England, mostly Orthodox in background and predominantely based in the London area. The New Commonwealth immigrants from South Asia brought with them their Islamic, Hindu, and Sikh traditions, and the English Muslim community is especially strong with about one million regular attendees at mosques. It is estimated that there may soon be more practicing Muslims in England than Christians. Occasional controversies have broken out in recent years because of clashes between traditional Islamic belief and the more permissive attitudes of secular Britain. One source of tension was English novelist Salman Rushdie's book, *The Satanic Verses*, which was deemed highly offensive by some Muslims.

Class

England was always traditionally one of the most class-conscious countries in the world. Its population was clearly divided into social strata that could be recognized by dress, speech, behavior, and attitudes. Someone was born working, middle, or upper class, and remained part of that group from cradle to grave. That, at least, was the old stereotype. Up until about forty years ago it remained a fairly accurate description of the way England's social structure was arranged. Class distinctions remained extremely rigid, and it was next to impossible to progress from one to another, even with money, because of the crucial differences in accent. "The English people are branded on the tongue," said George Orwell in the 1940s, by which he meant that the language someone used was always gave away their social origins. Power remained safely in the grip of people from "good" backgrounds, like the elite private schools and privileged universities.

The slow fading away of these distinctions had several causes. As the British economy shifted away from manufacturing to service industries, more clerical and "white-collar" jobs became available and so the ranks of the middle class grew larger. Educational opportunities at all levels improved, and attendance at Oxford or Cambridge was no longer the exclusive right of the well-born. Even sports and entertainment celebrities played their role by showing how birth was no necessary barrier to success— if the working-class Beatles from Liverpool could conquer the world in the 1960s, why couldn't other Britons from humble backgrounds also accomplish their dreams? The result was a steady decline in the importance of class as an indicator of a person's future prospects and opportunities.

This does not mean that class has become irrelevant in 21st century England, however. The highest political ranks continue to be disproportionately full of people from well-to-do and aristocratic families, and having the right social connections is still a big advantage in making a career. Qualifications and to some extent money have become much more important than breeding in today's England, but wearing the correct sort of old school tie still pays dividends.

The British monarch today is a figurehead with only ceremonial duties. Real political power is in the hands of Parliament and the prime minister. Still, the monarch does take part in many important government events. For example, Queen Elizabeth II is seen presiding over the opening session of Parliament in November 1995.

CHAPTER 5

Government

T he United Kingdom, of which England is a part, is unique amongst major world nations in having no written constitution. That does not mean to say that the country has no constitution at all; in fact, it has one of the oldest in the world. But it is not embodied in a single, formal document like the Constitution of the United States of America. Rather, it is a collection of laws and statutes, some official and some binding through the power of tradition and precedent. Although this might sound haphazard—and some Britons would agree that it is—it also has given the UK an unusual political stability, and its citizens have long enjoyed important civil liberties. England was one of the first modern countries in the world to give serious thought to democratic ideas and the rule of law. Many of the principles enshrined in the US Constitution, such as the "separation of powers" between different branches of government, have their origins in the unwritten UK constitution. The informal nature of British law also allows it to be flexible in response to change. Although some of the branches of government have apparently remained the same for centuries, like the monarchy, their real functions have changed beyond recognition.

The Monarchy

The British head of state, the supreme source of all political authority, is the monarch. Since 1952 that has been Queen Elizabeth II of the House of Windsor. As a child, Queen Elizabeth never expected to become monarch. Her father, the Duke of York, was only second in line to the throne after his elder brother Edward, the Prince of Wales. But in 1936, Edward VIII, as he had become, abdicated his position after less than a year because of his wish to marry an American divorcee, Wallis Simpson—an unpardonable act in those days. Elizabeth's father became king instead, reigning as George VI. King George was greatly respected by the British people for his courage during World War II, but the stress of unexpected public office was too much for him and he died relatively young. His eldest daughter Elizabeth, who was only 26 at the time of her father's death, was crowned Queen in a spectacular 1953 coronation ceremony that was broadcast around the world using the new technology of television. She has reigned ever since. In 2002 she marked her fiftieth year on the throne, her "Golden Jubilee."

In theory at least, the queen's powers are vast. She is the leader of all three branches of government (the executive, the legislature, and the judiciary), commander-in-chief of the armed forces, and head of the Church of England. All public officeholders and civil servants, including soldiers, sailors, and airmen, give a personal oath of loyalty to her. No law can be passed without her consent, and any important decision such as a declaration of war against another country must be made in her name alone. In earlier times these powers were quite real, and the monarch ruled almost unchecked by any constraint. In practice, however, the history of the British monarchy over the past several hundred years has been the steady reduction of its real decision-making role. Nowadays the Queen's influence is mostly nominal, and all genuine authority in the United Kingdom resides with the prime minister and his parliamentary government using "Crown Prerogative," meaning power exercised in the name of the queen.

This is not to say that the queen is irrelevant, however. She is the physical embodiment of British law and government, and is viewed as a vital symbol of the nation's stability. Her presence can be seen everywhere in British life; her image adorns every coin, banknote and stamp, and her royal coat of arms (with the Norman French motto Honi Soit Qui Mal Y Pense—"Evil to Him Who Thinks Ill of It") is displayed on thousands of public buildings. Queen Elizabeth opens every session of Parliament and reads "the Queen's Speech," which is a statement of the government's policy intentions and is really written by the prime minister. She is also the patron of hundreds of charitable organizations, makes ceremonial visits both throughout the United Kingdom and the rest of the world, and hosts garden parties at her official London home (Buckingham Palace) and other royal residences to honor special invited guests. She also has a separate role as the head of the Commonwealth of Nations, the international organization whose member-states are countries from the old British Empire. Queen Elizabeth has been an extremely hard-working and devoted monarch, and although there are increasing questions about the future of the institution (for which see below), she personally is widely admired in her own country as well as throughout the world.

Parliament

The British Parliament is also many hundreds of years old. It can trace its origins to the 1215 "Magna Carta," an agreement that forced King John (of Robin Hood fame) to take advice from his barons before making important political decisions. By the 13th century English kings would summon parliaments together in order to pass new taxes, but only on special occasions. Parliament did not sit as a regular branch of government until the early 17th century, when it became the focus of a long-running battle with the king that ultimately led to the Civil War and the Glorious Revolution. After William of Orange succeeded to the throne in 1688, it was recognized that Parliament, not the monarch, would now be the real center of government. Even so, it was not until the 20th century that kings and queens finally abandoned their pretences to power.

Parliament is located in Westminster, in the center of London. The modern building, with its famous clock tower containing the huge bell known as "Big Ben," was constructed in the mid-19th century after the original was destroyed by fire. Parliament is made up of two houses, the House of Commons and the House of Lords. The House of Commons is the main debating chamber, where laws are passed and crucial issues of the day discussed. Its members are known as "MPs," or Members of Parliament; as of 2002 there were 659 of them, each representing a regional con-stituency in England, Scotland, Wales or Northern Ireland. Nearly all MPs are members of a political party, and usually the largest single party in the House becomes the government, with its leader elected prime minister. The prime minister, who lives at a special public residence called 10 Downing Street, assembles a group of senior MPs from his or her own party to become Ministers in his or her government. This select group is known as the Cabinet. One of the unique features of the British constitutional system is that the prime minister and his cabinet, sometimes known as the executive or day-to-day policy branch of the state, are also part of the legislative or law-making branch. It is as if the American president was also an ordinary congressional representative as well the occupant of the White House. Although this might sound odd, in practice this system works efficiently enough.

The House of Lords has gone through extensive changes in

the last couple of years, and at the time of writing its future is still unclear. Traditionally, it is the seat of the "Lords Temporal" and the "Lords Spiritual"—meaning the great hereditary aristocrats of the realm and the bishops of the Church of England. It is also the House where the "Law Lords," the heads of the judicial branch of government, sit. The Lords used to have much the same powers as the House of Commons, but since the early 20th century its authority has been steadily diminishing. In 1911 the so-called Parliament Act removed the Lords' ability to veto new laws. More recently, the Lords has been criticized for being an undemocratic institution that rewards wealth and status with power. As a result, in 1999 the hereditary "Peers of the Realm," as most Lords members are known, lost their automatic right to sit and vote there. The present government is considering a plan to completely revamp the Lords and turn it into an elected chamber like the House of Commons, but this is still uncertain.

Political Parties

At least once every five years the House of Commons is adjourned, and its MPs are re-elected in a general election. This is a time of great political excitement in the United Kingdom, and each political party vies to get as large a percentage of the popular vote as it can. All British citizens over the age of 18 can vote in the constituency that they live in. There is no separate voting procedure for the executive branch; the prime minister has to be re-elected by his constituency residents, just like any other MP. It is even possible, though rare, for an important party member to lose his seat and thus be ineligible to take part in government even if his own side wins the election as a whole.

Currently there are three major political parties represented in the House of Commons. The party that won the 2001 general election with a huge majority—166 MPs more than all the other parties put together—was the Labour Party. Its leader, the prime minister as of 2002, is Tony Blair. Blair's party is over one hundred years old, and was formed by trade union representatives to give working-class voters a voice in Parliament. Traditionally, the Labour Party has adopted left-wing, socialist policies; it was Labour which introduced the extensive welfare state system after its historic parliamentary victory in 1945. However, after a series of electoral disasters in the 1980s and early 1990s, Labour's leadership slowly eased the party towards the political center. It reduced its involvement with the trade unions and dropped a number of increasingly unpopular proposals to nationalize important parts of the British economy. Tony Blair has been a great success at returning Labour to power, although critics within his own party complain that in seeking electoral success he has abandoned the principles on which the Labour movement was originally based.

The second largest party after the 2001 election with 166 MPs was the Conservative Party—sometimes known as the "Tories"—led by Iain Duncan Smith. The Conservatives, who as their name implies take a more cautious, right-of-center attitude towards issues, were the party of government throughout much of the 20th century. In 1979 their leader Margaret Thatcher became the first female prime minister in history, and she held this office for eleven years. Thatcher remains a controversial figure; although she made many important structural changes to British industry and so brought about a revival of the UK's flagging economy, her policies also caused high unemployment and opponents accused her of trying to destroy the welfare state. After her resignation in 1990 the new Conservative leader John Major became prime minister. Major was a less divisive figure than Thatcher, but internal differences in his party over membership in the European Union caused havoc for his administration and he suffered a humiliating defeat to Tony Blair in the general election of 1997.

The Liberal Democratic Party came third in the 2001

Tony Blair, who was elected prime minister as a member of the Labour Party, is seen here (at lower right), shaking hands with voters just after his victory. He and his party won a huge victory over the other major party, the Conservatives, in 1997 and 2001.

election with 52 MPs. "Lib-Dems,"as they are sometimes known, have a complex history. The old Liberal Party was a powerful force in British politics up to the World War I, when it went into a long, slow decline. In the early 1980s it was joined by a group of breakaway Labour MPs who were unhappy with their party's increasingly left wing stance. This parliamentary alliance resulted eventually in the founding of a new party. Under their current leader, Charles Kennedy, the Liberal Democrats campaign for stronger pro-European links, and they are equally committed to reforming the voting system that they argue discriminates against smaller parties such as themselves.

English Regional Government

While all the regions of the United Kingdom are represented similarly in Westminster, each has its own unique form of local government providing for police forces, fire brigades, healthcare, education, and so on. England is no exception to this. The English system is a rather intricate product of centuries of overlapping laws and traditions. Until as recently as the early 1970s, much of England was still governed by administrative units dating back to the Anglo-Saxons and the Normans. The three main bodies were, in increasing order of size, the parish, the borough, and the county (or shire). Parishes were small church districts that originally had a responsibility to provide welfare to old and poor residents. They were in turn organized into boroughs, both rural and urban, which had their own courts of law and local government officials. During the 19th century, borough councils developed with elected representatives. Finally there were the 40 shire counties, some extremely big like Yorkshire (which was so large that it was subdivided into three "ridings," north, east, and west) and some tiny like Huntingdonshire. The monarch's personal representatives in each county were the Lord Lieutenant and the royal sheriff, whose jobs were to enforce the King's law.

Parishes, boroughs and counties all continue to exist. But the local government reorganization of 1972 changed many of their boundaries and functions. Some historic counties like Westmoreland and Rutland vanished, while new ones such as Humberside and Cumbria appeared. Metropolitan counties, representing large urban units like Manchester and Birmingham, were created. These changes remain controversial to this day, and there has been much tinkering with the system since the 1970s. The biggest complaint has been over county boundary changes. Counties have always been more than just bland administrative units; they have strong local traditions and inspire a fierce loyalty in their residents, just as States do in the U.S. People born and raised in one county are very unhappy to be told that they now live in another, however "rational" such reorganization might seem from the viewpoint of Westminster.

London has unique arrangements of its own. The original Roman city of London was only one square mile in size, bordered on all sides by a defensive wall. For centuries afterwards this tiny area—known as "the City"—was technically the extent of London's jurisdiction. The City today has virtually no residents, but contains many banks and financial institutions and such landmarks as St. Paul's Cathedral and the Tower of London. Its medieval guilds continue to elect an honorary Mayor who has important ceremonial functions but no real administrative power. As London grew it became increasingly obvious that these antique provisions were unsatisfactory. A larger county of London was created, but the city continued to expand into neighboring Middlesex, Kent, and Surrey. In 1963 Greater London, encompassing over 7 million people divided into 32 boroughs, appeared on the map. Twenty three years later Greater London's Council was abolished by the government of Margaret Thatcher, leaving the city the only metropolis in the world without any unified city government. This was rectified in 2000 with the appointment of Greater London's first directly elected mayor, Ken Livingstone.

Political Reform?

As we can see, the British constitution is a sometimes-bewildering assortment of laws and institutions old and new, with recent innovations alongside thousand-year-old customs. Although there is much continuity to the system, it has always been subject to reform and change. In the 17th and 18th centuries, Parliament enforced its rights against the power of the monarch. In the Victorian era the House of Commons was opened up to larger membership and voting privileges based on property ownership were repealed. During the 20th century women also won the right to vote, the influence of the

During her administration in the 1980s, Prime Minister Margaret Thatcher abolished the city government of Greater London. Thatcher, seen here waving outside the prime minister's official residence at 10 Downing Street, London, was elected in May 1979 to be the first female prime minister of Great Britain.

House of Lords was steadily reduced, and local government was reorganized. Now, critics of the UK's current political arrangements believe that further reforms appropriate to a new century are also required.

In 1977, at the time of Queen Elizabeth's Silver Jubilee celebrating her 25th year on the throne, the position of the British monarchy seemed unassailable. Now a significant minority of the population has indicated in opinion polls that it would like to see a presidential republic take over after the current queen's death. There are several reasons for the decline in deference towards the Royal Family, including the controversy that surrounded the late Princess Diana and her failed marriage to Charles, the Prince of Wales. Throughout its history the monarchy's popularity has ebbed and flowed, and just because it is currently going through a troubled period does not necessarily mean that it is doomed. The majority of Britons continue to support the idea of a constitutional monarch, if for no other reason than its value for the tourist trade. But it is probable that future kings and queens will take a more low-key approach to their role, abandoning some of the expensive pomp and ceremony and emulating the modest "bicycling monarchs" of the Netherlands and Scandinavia.

Westminster's powerful centralized role has also been under fire in recent years, especially from people in Scotland, Wales, and Northern Ireland. They complain that the "British" state is really just the English state under an assumed name, and that England dominates the United Kingdom to their disadvantage. In defense of the current system some politicians have claimed that this injustice is more mythical than real; the other UK regions are over-represented in the House of Commons by population size, they point out, and non-English citizens tend to receive higher state benefits per person than the English. It is undeniable, however, that Parliament's physical location in London, and the unfortunate tendency by English people to ignore their neighbors' complaints, has caused much resentment. The recent creation of parliaments in Edinburgh and Cardiff, and the new Northern Irish government, may allay some of these criticisms for now. But the long-term survival of the United Kingdom in its present form is by no means guaranteed.

England has historically been one of the richest and most powerful nations in the world. This 1808 painting shows a group of well-to-do businessmen gathering at the coal exchange in London. Since that time, England's economy has continued to expand, although it has suffered severe recessions and other difficulties over the years.

CHAPTER

6

Economy

The United Kingdom is one of the richest countries in the world. In 2000 its Gross Domestic Product (GDP), a standard measure of national wealth, was $1.36 trillion, making the UK one of only four European countries with a GDP of over one thousand billion U.S. dollars. Britain is a founding member of the "G-8" group of advanced industrial nations that meets periodically to discuss world economic policy. It imports and exports goods and services worth hundreds of billions of dollars every year, and is one of the United States' half-dozen most important trading partners. England, as the largest and most populous region of the UK, is the main contributor to this financial powerhouse, and its capital city London is the focus of England's wealth.

Britain's economic performance has not always been a source of pride, however. In the 1970s, the UK was sometimes referred to as "the sick man of Europe"' because of its flagging production output, high unemployment, and rampaging inflation. As the world's first industrial nation it was also one of the first countries to undergo the harsh realities of "deindustrialization," as its old manufacturing base was dismantled under the pressure of new foreign competition. The UK is a good example of what is called a post-industrial nation, a country that has built up and lost its heavy industry and replaced it with a predominantly service-oriented economy. Modern Britain's greatest economic opportunity, but also its biggest dilemma, is its continued role within the European Union (EU), as that organization proceeds with monetary and political unification.

Natural Resources

England, at the brink of the Industrial Revolution in the mid-1700s, had the perfect natural resources to create a modern factory-based economy. Its forests of broad-leaved and conifer trees provided an excellent source of timber for the burgeoning shipbuilding industry, while its rock, gravel, and sand quarries, as well as its reserves of clay and salt, were necessary ingredients for manufacturing industry. Above all, the green fields of England were built on coal—lots of coal. Huge underground reserves in Tyneside, Yorkshire, and Nottinghamshire were mined for their vital "black gold," which powered English steamships across the globe and kept the country's railroads, iron, and steel works running. The city of Newcastle in northeastern England produced and distributed so much coal that the phrase "sending coals to Newcastle" became a stock expression for a pointless activity.

England still has a significant timber and mineral industry, but over the last hundred years it has steadily shrunk in importance as its resources have dwindled and cheaper foreign alternatives have become available. The story of the coal industry is especially sad. As English coal became increasingly uncompetitive on the world market in the 1970s and 1980s, the governments of the day sought to restructure the mining sector and close down the least profitable pits. This provoked a dispute with the powerful National Union of Mineworkers (NUM) that led to a bitter year-long strike in 1984–1985. Ultimately the government prevailed and most of England's remaining coal mines were closed down during the following decade. This left many communities destitute, especially in northern England, and remains a source of great anger amongst former mineworkers.

Despite the eclipse of coal, the UK continues to be an unusually large producer of energy resources, with about 10 percent of its GDP being energy-related—the highest share of any major industrial nation. This is because of the discovery of large oil and natural gas reserves in the North Sea during the 1970s. These oil and gas fields lie under the seabed in what is one of the roughest stretches of water in the world, and require specially engineered offshore platforms to tap into the rich natural resources below the waves. For months on end, drillers live on these lonely man-made islands pumping oil and gas back to the mainland. North Sea energy has brought in valuable government revenues, but Britain's power needs far exceed what can be extracted from offshore waters and the country remains dependent on imported fuels for most of its electrical power production. Some alternative energy initiatives have been attempted. The world's first commercial atomic power station was opened at Calder Hall in northwest England in 1956, and the UK continues to have a string of nuclear reactors as part of its national energy system; however, fears about their safety have discouraged large-scale investment. Some attempts to utilize solar, wind, and wave power are ongoing, but as yet have not become important sources of Britain's energy.

Agriculture and Fishing

One of the most distinctive features of the English landscape, especially seen from above in an airplane, is a patchwork quilt of irregular fields that cover the countryside. England's farming economy went through an early rationalization process from the 1500s onwards known as the "Enclosures," and this combined the tiny strips of medieval farmland into larger, more efficient units. But the British never developed the enormous field systems that are found in the prairie states of the US and Canada, and by North American standards English agriculture is very unevenly organized. This is not to say that it is unproductive, however. On the contrary, England's farming industry is probably the most well organized in Europe, and the country produces 60 percent of its food needs using only one hundredth of the total labor force. England's fertile lowlands have always been the best part of the United Kingdom for farming, and the introduction of mechanization in the 20th century made England largely self-reliant in wheat, barley, and potatoes (incidentally, one of the confusing things for American visitors to England is that wheat is often called corn). Market gardening, or the growing of fruits, flowers, and vegetables, is especially popular in southern England. The county of Kent is traditionally known as the "Garden of England" and is famous for its orchards and flowerbeds. Some parts of the southwest are warm enough all season to plant vineyards and bottle wine.

Just as the English sometimes (rather impolitely) call their French neighbors the "frogs" because of their reputed taste for frogs legs, so the French have traditionally called the English the "Roast Beefs." This indicates how important the cattle industry has historically been, not just for England's economy, but for the country's whole way of life and self-image. In the early 1990s worrying reports began to emerge that Britain's cow herds were infected with a mysterious, crippling virus known as BSE, or mad cow disease. Even worse, medical evidence showed that in rare circumstances it was possible to transfer this disease to humans who ate the infected beef. The BSE scare resulted in Britain's beef exports being banned across Europe and North America, and 4.5 million cattle had to be slaughtered to expunge the disease from the country's herds. If

One of the scariest problems England has faced in recent memory is the threat of mad cow disease, a virus that can cause a rare, severe brain disease in those who eat the meat of infected cows. In the 1990s, about 4.5 million cows were slaughtered to stop the spread of the disease, although English Health Secretary Stephen Dorrell said in March 1996 that the government would consider killing all British cattle—some 11 million—if necessary.

this were not bad enough for livestock farmers, in 2001 an equally devastating infection called "foot and mouth" disease broke out in sheep and pig farms across the UK. The government took drastic action, ordering the slaughter of almost 4 million more animals to prevent the further spread of the infection. These twin disasters have done enormous damage to Britain's livestock industry and it will take decades for the country's farmers to recover.

The recent story of England's fishing industry also is not a happy one. For centuries, deep-sea fishermen based in ports like Lowestoft, Great Yarmouth, and Grimsby have battled the tempestuous waters of the Atlantic Ocean and the North Sea to bring in the catch of cod, haddock, whiting, and other saltwater fish. Fish has traditionally been an important part of the English diet, and "fish 'n' chips"—battered fish and fries—is a regular choice on the national dinner plate. But overfishing by large mechanized trawlers has dangerously depleted fish stocks in the seas surrounding the British Isles, and the European Union's rigid quotas on the amount of fish that can now be landed every year has made it difficult for fishermen to remain in business. The future of the fishing industry is very uncertain.

Manufacturing and Heavy Industry

In the 19th century, Prime Minister Benjamin Disraeli described Britain as the workshop of the world. This was not an idle boast; Britain, by virtue of being the first industrialized country on the planet, was the single biggest source of all manufacturing and heavy industrial goods. The UK's products were sold to every continent, and British inventors dreamed up many of the machines and devices that we take for granted in the modern world: the steam engine, the railroad, the telephone, television, and the computer, to name but a few. Manchester, in northern England, was the world's first industrial city and the model for all subsequent factory-based towns.

By the end of the World War II in 1945, many of the country's older industries were feeling the pinch of low productivity and fierce international competition. The post-war Labour Party government nationalized large industries like steelmaking, but this did not prevent their long-term decline. In 1979 Margaret Thatcher's Conservative administration came into power and introduced a tough monetary policy that made it very difficult for many of the UK's older and more inefficient manufacturers to remain in business. Hundreds of thousands of factory jobs were lost, both private and state-run, and over the next decade the Thatcher government sold most of the UK's remaining public industries into private hands.

At the start of the 21st century England is much less reliant on manufacturing and traditional heavy industry than it was even twenty years ago. Nonetheless, one in five of its workers is still in the manufacturing sector. Those firms that survived the brutal cull of the 1980s tended to be in hi-tech areas like microelectronics, aircraft production, chemical, and pharmaceuticals. Older crafts like brewing, textiles, and paper and glass production still exist, but on a smaller scale. England's shipbuilding, motorbike, and car industries have largely disappeared, although a few highly specialist firms like Rolls-Royce survive because of the prestige of their products.

Services

What has largely replaced manufacturing as the hub of the UK's economy is the service sector. Services span everything from banking and insurance to tourism, and from retail to the entertainment industry. About two-thirds of the English work force is now part of the service sector, and this proportion continues to grow. London was at one time the world's most important financial center, and "the City" in the capital's business district continues to be a key global marketplace, particularly for precious metals like gold and silver. The London Stock Exchange, founded in 1773, ranks alongside Wall Street and the stock markets of Frankfurt, Hong Kong, and Tokyo as a focus for international share and bond trading. An even older institution is the insurance broker Lloyds, which opened its doors for the first time in 1688 and has been the world's main shipping underwriter for over three centuries.

Tourism has become one of the UK's most vital money-earners, with earnings estimated at over $100 billion in 2000. Around 25 million people visit Britain every year, predominantly from the United States and elsewhere in Europe; needless to say, catering to this massive influx of guests has become a major task for the national economy. England's part in this annual migration to the UK is a vital one, because of the country's large number of desirable tourist attractions. London, with its historical landmarks, vibrant nightlife, and famous theater traditions is a natural starting-point for travelers to the UK. But every region of England enjoys a rich variety of scenic beauty and sightseeing opportunities. Homegrown tourism is also important. Traditionally, the English like to "be beside the seaside" on their summer vacations, and they flock to shore resorts like Brighton, Blackpool, and Bridlington. The fickleness of the English weather means that these towns can't compete with Spain or Florida for sunshine, but they are an ingrained part of the English vacation experience.

No survey of English services would be complete without a mention of the music business. Ever since the so-called British Invasion of the United States in the 1960s by bands like the Beatles and the Rolling Stones, popular music has been an important national revenue source. Fashions come and go, but English singers and bands continue to do very well abroad, especially in the vital American market. Where once John Lennon and Mick Jagger flew the flag, now Oasis, Radiohead, and Robbie Williams help to support Britain's balance of trade.

Transportation and Trade

England is a relatively small country and is well served by a modern transportation network. The three major airports in the London area, Heathrow, Gatwick, and Stansted, together handle over 40 million passengers each year, either visitors to the UK or travelers continuing on to other destinations. In the 1960s the government began a major road-building program that linked up the UK's cities by a motorway (interstate) service traversing the country. Car use is common among Britons, and traffic congestion has become a serious economic as well as environmental problem in recent years. Many urban areas are adopting "pedestrianization," or the closing off of city centers to automobile traffic, as one way of cutting back on the pollution and frustration caused by too many cars on the road. To encourage travel by other means, some towns have revamped their bus services and have even brought back trolley cars,

England is a small country with a fairly large population, and when those people take to the roads, traffic congestion can become a serious issue. To try to make travel easier, the government began a road-building program in the 1960s. This 1969 photograph shows a highway overpass under construction.

which had largely disappeared from English roadways by the 1950s. Bicycle use is also common, and in addition to its exercise value a bike can be a good way of getting round England's complex and narrow city streets. Londoners are particularly fortunate in that they can rely on the capital's famous underground, or "tube" service. The rest of the UK has a widespread railroad network, but since its privatization in the 1990s many commuters have complained that the service has deteriorated and a number of high-profile accidents have damaged the industry's reputation for safety.

Until 1994 the only way to reach Great Britain from abroad was by air or by sea. This changed that year when the Channel Tunnel between Folkestone on the Kent Coast and Calais was opened by Queen Elizabeth and the French president. The

Chunnel, as it is known, provides the first British land bridge to the European mainland since the end of the Ice Age. Although both countries had talked about such a tunnel since the 19th century, fears of military invasion and the engineering difficulties involved kept all plans strictly on the drawing board until the 1980s. Even now many Britons are concerned about the increase in drug smuggling and illegal immigration that the Chunnel is bringing, as well as the possibility of catastrophic terrorist attack. The age-old concern about the spread of the disease rabies, which is unknown in Great Britain, still means that all pets entering the UK have to endure months of quarantine before they can be let free.

Trade remains a very important factor in the British economy. In 2000 the UK imported $324 billion worth of goods and exported $282 billion, chiefly to other European Union members but also to the United States and Japan. The country makes up in part this trade deficit by the "invisible" earnings it receives from financial services like banking, stock broking, and insurance in the City of London. Dividends from business investments in other countries are also very important in keeping the account books balanced. Throughout the early 20th century Britain had the largest merchant marine of any nation, which it used to carry its trade across the world's oceans. Shipping losses in the two world wars and the gradual replacement of sea by air transport whittled away at this mighty fleet, and nowadays relatively few vessels continue to fly the "Red Ensign," although there are still some high-profile ships like the luxury liner Queen Elizabeth II (QEII).

The European Question

Britain's economic future will be dominated by its relationship with the European Union (EU), which it joined in 1973. The question of the Common Market, as it used to be known, has played a key role in the country's politics for over twenty-five years and has dogged governments of all political parties.

When it was originally set up, the EU—then called the EEC, or European Economic Community—was intended to be a free-trade area for western European nations, a means of bringing their national economies together and discouraging the kind of cross-border tensions that had led to the wars of 1914 and 1939. Over time other, more ambitious, goals developed. In 1991 its members signed the Maastricht Agreement, which committed them to a timetable for monetary union by the end of the decade. The United Kingdom was unenthusiastic about this plan and opted to remain out of the single European currency, although it stayed in the EU. This new currency, the Euro, was unveiled at the beginning of 2002 and now most of the EU's members have adopted it as their national monetary unit. This leaves Britain in a dilemma. The majority of the British public remains unconvinced about the merits of the single currency and many members of Parliament are fiercely opposed to its introduction. On the other hand, if Britain clings to the pound for too long, then the other EU members may become impatient with the UK's excessive caution and press ahead without the British; they might even demand that Britain leave the Union. Critics of the EU back in England would be delighted with this result, of course!

As of 2002, no decision by the ruling Labour Party has been made. The Government minister responsible for financial affairs, the Chancellor of the Exchequer Gordon Brown, has laid down certain financial conditions that must be met before he will consider opting for the Euro. In any case, a national referendum on the subject is now virtually certain. The outcome will have a decisive effect on the future economic development of the UK, and it will be fascinating to see what choice Britons eventually take.

England remains a major player in international affairs. After terrorists attacked the United States in September 2001, England took part in the worldwide effort to defeat the terrorists in Afghanistan. Prime Minister Tony Blair is seen here in October 2001, explaining that British forces would be joining the United States in the war on terrorism.

Living in England Today

ngland has experienced the same kind of changes in the make-up of family life as North America over the past fifty years. Older, more traditional forms of extended family, where many generations lived closely together—even under the same roof—gave way to smaller nuclear families with two adult parents and perhaps one or two children. Nuclear families in turn have broken down with the rapid rise in divorce, single parenthood, and living together outside of marriage. Some conservative critics argue that these trends are the result of a permissive society in which too much tolerance towards alternative living styles has resulted in broken homes, juvenile delinquency, and teenage pregnancy. There are indeed many valid concerns about the direction of some English social trends. Violent crime, though much lower than in the United States, has risen dramatically since World War II, while the divorce rate has skyrocketed and the number of young unmarried mothers has increased many times over. However, others point out these regrettable developments are the inevitable result of more deep-seated economic changes, experienced in all advanced industrial nations, and that in practice there is little that society can do about them. Their significance also may be exaggerated, also. Although there is much alarmism in the national media about the imminent "collapse of civilization," England remains a largely peaceful, law-abiding country with a surprisingly resilient respect for older social customs.

Until 1918 women in England were denied the vote (something that was challenged by an extremely noisy and often violent "Suffragette" movement) and had few vocational opportunities other than motherhood, domestic service, and a few niche industries like textiles. During the two world wars women poured into the factories to replace men called up to the army, and their contribution to the war effort left a lasting mark on gender roles. More and more women entered the workforce, including the legal and health professions, in the post-war period. In 1979, when Margaret Thatcher was elected prime minister, the UK was almost unique in having both a female head of state (the Queen) and head of government. Despite these high-profile successes, however, many English women still complain that they are underpaid relative to men and that they remain burdened with too many of their traditional household duties during marriage. The lack of good state-subsidized nursery facilities is a bone of contention for younger working women, who are often faced with the dilemma of maintaining their careers, or becoming full-time mothers.

Health and Welfare

In 1945 a Labour Party government was elected with a mandate from the voters to create Britain's first comprehensive health and social security system, something that became known as the "Welfare State." Before World War II, Britain had been blighted by crippling poverty and unemployment in many depressed industrial areas. There was a determination by the new political class to knock down the urban slums and replace them with better housing and facilities for working people. Post-war local councils built hundreds of thousands of new homes, many of them publicly owned and available to new residents for a low rent. They also embarked on the large-scale construction of high-rise apartment blocks, which unfortunately often became as ill kempt and dangerous as the 19th century slums they had replaced. A national insurance scheme for all workers was introduced, by which old age and disability pensions, unemployment benefits, and payments for low-earning families were guaranteed to everyone who contributed from their pay-packets. This social security scheme remains largely in place today, although it has been much revised to take into account growing costs and the problems of bureaucratic inefficiency. Its enduring popularity with the electorate prevented prime ministers like Margaret Thatcher, who was unconvinced about the wisdom of the Welfare State, from interfering too much with its structure. However, the changes in the British population's age demographics that we noted in Chapter 4 will make it very difficult to maintain the current system without a drastic increase in funding. More and more elderly people will have to be supported by a relatively shrinking workforce.

Perhaps the most important achievement of the Welfare State reforms was the creation in 1948 of the National Health Service, or NHS. This committed the British state for the first time in history to providing free on-demand health care for the entire population "from cradle to grave," as the saying went. Nothing in this world is really free, of course, and taxpayers had to provide for the cost of the NHS through their national insurance contributions.

But the guarantee that medical care would henceforth be provided to ordinary people without considering their ability to pay was a major breakthrough in public health, and one that Britons remain proud of to this day. Like the rest of the Welfare State system, the NHS has had to adapt to changing conditions in the 21st century. The expansion of its role as medical science advances and the population ages has put it under great pressure to deliver quality care, and there have been complaints that a service, once envied around the world, has become underfunded, administratively bloated, and inefficient. Private medical care, which is available at an extra cost, has become a more popular option in recent years.

Education

The third plank of the Welfare State after social security and health was a new education system, actually brought in a little earlier by the wartime Conservative government in 1944. The structure of primary and secondary education in England and Wales—Scotland has its own procedures—has changed often since the war, and remains in flux today. Broadly speaking, the current organization is as follows. All children are required to attend school between the ages of five and sixteen. When they get to age 11, they usually transfer from a primary to a secondary, or "comprehensive" school. In the old system students took an exam at this point and either qualified to attend a grammar school, with the intention of eventually going to university, or a less academically prestigious secondary-modern school. Nowadays the two types of school have been combined (a point that still generates much criticism from traditional educators). At the age of 16 pupils take their GCSE, or General Certificate exams. They are free to leave school at this point to find employment, but increasingly many students stay on for another two years in the equivalent of high school, known in England as the "Sixth Form", to take "A" or Advanced level exams. If their A-levels are good enough then they can go on to college.

The two great higher learning institutions of England are the universities of Oxford and Cambridge, founded in 1167 and 1209 respectively. Both are world-famous for the quality of education they provide, and students from across the UK and indeed the globe vie for the opportunity to study there. There are over 80 other colleges and universities across the UK, all of which are nominally independent, but in practice (with one exception, the University of Buckingham) rely on state funds. There is also the so-called Open University, which was developed in the 1960s to allow adults to obtain a degree by distance learning. Until the early 1990s university students received generous government stipends and free tuition to provide for them during their studies. More recently, tuition payments have been levied directly and grants replaced by student loans, although the cost of good college education in England remains much lower than it is in the United States.

Although a very small number of pupils attend them, a word must be said about England's famous private schools like Eton and Harrow, which have become internationally famous through fictional works like *Tom Brown's Schooldays*. Confusingly, these fee-charging institutions are known in the UK as "public" schools—this dates back from the medieval period when most rich families educated their children using private tutors. These public schools were in their way the first type of national school system available to ordinary middle-class parents. At one time virtually the whole of England's social and political elite went through this handful of schools, which despite their high fees were often barbarously run. Now their influence has declined greatly, though former public schoolboys and girls remain disproportionately represented at Oxford and Cambridge.

Sports and Leisure

England is a nation of sports fanatics, and was the birth-place of three of the most popular games in the world—soccer, rugby, and cricket. Professional soccer—called football in England—is by the far the best-loved game of all, and hundreds of thousands of fans regularly attend matches by England's prestigious teams like Manchester United, Liverpool, and Arsenal. The English national squad has only won the World Cup once, in 1966, and this event is remembered fondly by all soccer-loving citizens. Rugby is a 19th-century derivative of soccer in which players are allowed to use their hands, and it is divided into professional Rugby League and amateur Rugby Union rules. The Six Nations tournament between England, Scotland, Wales, Ireland, France, and Italy is one of the key dates on the rugby calendar. Cricket is not that well known in the United States, but it is enormously popular in many parts of the former British Empire like India, Pakistan, Australia, New Zealand, and the Caribbean. Its complex rules defy simple explanation, but it is a game similar to baseball in which the object is to pitch (or bowl) the opposing batsman out. Modern English cricket fans take an almost ghoulish pleasure in seeing their national side consistently defeated by other teams. Other sports that are very popular in England include horse racing, snooker (similar to billiards), darts, Grand Prix racing, and tennis, especially the annual international tournament at Wimbledon near London.

There are almost as many leisure activities in England as there are people, but some of the better known are freshwater fishing, hiking (or "rambling"), golf, and gardening. Less energetic pursuits include gambling, either at shore-town bingo halls and at the racetrack or via the new National Lottery; trips to the local pub; and weekend adventures camping or staying at bed and breakfast hotels in the countryside.

Rugby is a derivative of soccer in which players can use their hands, and English professional teams play on a world-class level. This photograph was taken during an international match that pitted England against South Africa in December 2000. England won the game by a score of 25–17.

The English are renowned for being a nation of eccentric hobbyists, with thousands of weird and wonderful diversions such as crossword puzzles, mystery novels, ballroom dancing, stamp collecting, and train spotting. One of the charms of English life is the rich culture of private enthusiasms that people enjoy either alone or through clubs and societies.

Media and Entertainment

The British Broadcasting Corporation, or BBC, is the principal television and radio company in the UK. The BBC exists by royal charter, its board of directors is appointed by the state, and it receives its funding from a government-enforced license fee on all television sets. Nonetheless, it retains complete editorial independence from the authorities. Over the 80 years of its existence, the BBC has earned a worldwide reputation for the quality of its news and entertainment programming, and its radio World Service is listened to across the globe. The BBC's main competition comes from the Independent Television (ITV), which was established in the 1950s to provide a commercially funded alternative. Unlike the BBC, which carries no advertisements, the ITV channels pay their way by selling advertising slots during program breaks. Both the BBC and ITV have come under pressure recently from satellite television companies such as Sky, which was established to Australian media tycoon Rupert Murdoch.

Murdoch is also the owner of a large number of English newspapers, most famously the *Times,* which is one of the oldest and most influential papers in the world. Traditionally, England's newspapers were published in Fleet Street in London, but electronic printing techniques have encouraged many papers to move beyond this cramped location to more spacious and modern sites. The British press is usually divided into "broadsheet" and "tabloid" categories; the broadsheets like the *Telegraph* and the *Guardian* are larger and more serious papers, while tabloids such as the *Sun* and the *Mirror* are packed with lurid and sensational stories about celebrities, royalty, scandals, and gossip. There are also a number of important political and literary magazines published in London such as the *Economist*, the *New Statesman* and the *Spectator*.

Movies are very popular in England, either rented for VCR and DVD players or shown at big-screen cinemas. Hollywood blockbusters tend to dominate the listings, though there is a small but quietly successful homegrown movie industry that produces high-quality films. England has produced many internationally famous film stars, from Charlie Chaplin to Jude Law and Kate Winslet, but they tend to gravitate across the Atlantic to make their name in the United States rather than stay in the UK.

Traditions and Festivals

England has a rich folklore populated by legendary heroes and villains, some of whom are fictional, but loosely based on real persons. King Arthur of Camelot and the Knights of the Round Table fame was probably inspired by an authentic Romano-British monarch from the early Dark Ages who fought against the invading Anglo-Saxons, although obviously his story became much romanticized over time. Similarly, Robin Hood may have begun life as a Saxon bandit operating out of the wild northern forests like Sherwood in Nottinghamshire in defiance of King John's authority. Merry Men aside, it is extremely unlikely that he gave away much of his loot from the rich to the poor outside of ballads, however! A more recent example of a hero-outlaw is the 18th century highwayman Dick Turpin, who was definitely a real historical figure caught and hanged for his many stagecoach robberies in 1739. According to popular tradition, Turpin was a chivalrous rogue of the Jesse James variety; in reality, however, he seems to have been a ruthless criminal who had few compunctions about killing anyone who got in his way.

As a predominantly Christian country, England shares many of the same religiously based holidays and celebrations as the United States. English children eagerly await the arrival of Santa Claus like their American counterparts, although he's known there as "Father Christmas." Popular Yuletide foods include roast goose, steamed Christmas pudding, and mince pies. At the Christmas dinner table all the guests pull "crackers" with one another, small paper tubes containing a black powder strip that sparks noisily when the cracker is ripped open. The day after Christmas, December 26, is known in England as Boxing Day. This derives from an old tradition of tradesmen going from door to door collecting their Christmas boxes, or gifts, from grateful customers. Nowadays the custom has fallen out of fashion, but Boxing Day continues to be a national holiday on which post-Christmas sports matches are often scheduled.

One unique English celebration is Guy Fawkes' Night, or Bonfire Night as it's sometimes known, held every November 5. This is the celebration of the foiling of a plot to murder King James I and his members of Parliament in 1605; the conspirators hired an assassin, Guy Fawkes, to hide barrels of gunpowder in the cellar under the House of Lords. Fortunately for the King and his nobles the plot was uncovered and Guy Fawkes was publicly executed. This somewhat grisly spectacle is repeated across the country every November when children build bonfires and put an effigy, "the Guy," on the top. It is also the day traditionally when English people have fireworks ceremonies. Each year they sing:

> Remember, remember, the 5th of November,
> Gunpowder, Treason, and Plot!

There are many celebrations connected with the British royal family. The Queen is unique in having two birthdays,

Guy Fawkes' Night is one of England's most unique national holidays. It celebrates the day in November when a plot to kill King James I was discovered and stopped. Today, the day is celebrated with parties and fireworks, like these that took place in Somerset, England, in 1996.

her real one (April 21) and her official one on the second Saturday in June. On her official birthday, there is a magnificent ceremony at Horse Guards Parade in London called Trooping the Colour, when she inspects the flags or "colours" of one of the British army's foot guard regiments. More regularly, the Queen's official London residence, Buckingham Palace, is host to a ceremony called the Changing of the Guard, when the soldiers standing on sentry duty outside the Palace are relieved from duty. These troops wear the ceremonial scarlet jackets of Guardsmen and the large bearskin caps called "busbies."

Food

English food has acquired a rather bad reputation over the years. Admittedly, some of the more bizarre names for dishes like toad-in-the-hole (sausages in batter), spotted dick (spongy steamed pudding), and bangers and mash (more sausages, this time with mashed potatoes) can sound a bit off-putting. However, England can boast plenty of tasty original food. The traditional English breakfast of eggs, bacon, sausage, baked beans, fried mushrooms and so on is a treat for the taste-buds, although not perhaps the healthiest or most practical start to the morning. Roast dinners of beef, chicken, or ham, with vegetables, potatoes and Yorkshire Puddings (pancake batter cooked in small pudding basins) as side dishes are equally popular later in the day. The English love to combine meats with pastries, creating such delicacies as sausage rolls (sausage meat in a flaky pastry) and pork pies. English cheeses like Cheddar, Stilton, Lancashire, and Wensleydale are justifiably world-renowned for their quality. Battered cod, plaice, or haddock and "chips" (fries) can be bought almost anywhere, and "kippers," or smoked herrings, are also popular fish. The influence of New Commonwealth immigration is visible in the large number of Indian restaurants and Chinese fast-food stores that now proliferate across England's towns and cities.

The English have two liquid vices—beer and tea. English beer, known as "bitter," is traditionally drunk at room temperature and has a smooth, rich taste. Although the UK has mostly gone metric in recent years, it is still considered sacred to serve beer in pints and half-pints in English pubs. The English love of afternoon tea is well known. As well as the beverage itself, no "high tea" would be complete without scones lashed with thick Devonshire cream and jelly, cucumber sandwiches, or cookies. After tasting a delicious custard tart or slice of plum cake, few people can honestly say again that all English food is boring!

Today, England is one of the world's most powerful nations, as it has been for hundreds of years. With its stable government, centered at Parliament Square (seen here), and its centuries-old traditions, it is likely to continue to be a world leader in the years to come.

8

England Looks Ahead

In 1962, the U.S. Secretary of State, Dean Acheson, famously remarked that: "Great Britain has lost an Empire, and not yet found a role." By this he meant that the UK was still basking in its old imperial glory, even though all its colonies were fast disappearing, and was finding it difficult to adjust to the new reality of being an ordinary, middle-sized European country. In the same way, it might be possible to say that England in the 21st century is losing its little empire—the United Kingdom—without yet finding an alternative role. This is not an entirely new development. As was noted earlier, one large part of the British Isles, southern Ireland, left the UK in 1922. However, the increasing desire of the other parts of the United Kingdom—Scotland, Wales, and Northern Ireland—for greater political autonomy has put the long-term future of the UK in its present form in some doubt. What will this mean for England, traditionally the heartland of the "British" idea?

It may be too early to completely write off the UK as a nation-state. Although the Scots, Welsh, and Northern Irish have made it clear that they would like a greater say in the day-to-day workings of their own regions, there is as yet no majority in any one of them for complete independence. Membership of the United Kingdom has economic and political benefits as well as costs, and there is plenty of residual loyalty towards the old institutions of the state, especially the Royal Family. Many men and women who remember the fight for Britain during the 20th century's two world wars remain fiercely proud of their links to the UK. Regional parliaments may actually have pacified the demand for complete independence. It will be interesting to see if the pro-separatist political parties in the "Celtic fringe," as the non-English parts of the UK are sometimes called, continue to make headway in the new century.

Whether Britain survives or not as a concept, it seems clear that regional identities within the UK are becoming more important. Where does this leave England? As the people at the heart of the British state, the English have to some extent diluted their own national consciousness in favor of a larger British identity. For example, the English patron saint, the dragon-slayer St. George, has his saint's day on April 23 every year. But there are no organized celebrations of this day in the same way that there are for St. Andrew of Scotland, St. David of Wales, or St. Patrick of Ireland. Many English people are not even aware of the correct date of St. George's Day. Another example is the national anthem that is played at international soccer matches; the Scottish, Welsh and Northern Irish teams have special anthems of their own, but the England squad uses the general British anthem "God Save the Queen." For many years, English soccer fans waved the Union Jack at their games, rather than the more technically correct Cross of St. George (the horizontal and vertical red cross on a white background at the center of the Union Jack). Small details like this demonstrate how Britain and England have become synonymous in people's minds, including many of the English themselves.

Symbols aside, there is also the more practical question of England and the rest of the UK's relationship with the United States and Europe. For decades presidents and prime ministers have spoken of the special relationship between the US and the UK based on ties of language, custom, and wartime and peacetime alliances. On the other hand, Britain is increasingly connected to events taking place in the European Union, which with its recent creation of a single currency seems to be moving inexorably towards greater federal union. These competing relationships leave the UK's future path unclear. Imperial Britain's old ability to remain friendly but aloof from both continents is now next to impossible, but it remains to be seen whether the country can juggle its North American and European interests at the same time without having to commit to one or the other.

The 20th century was a period of almost constant decline of England's international power and prestige, and with the survival of the British political union looking a great deal less certain, at least in its present form, one might be tempted to guess that the 21st century will be a grim epoch for England. But that is taking much too pessimistic a view. England's role may change, but whatever happens it will remain an important country with a unique and precious culture all of its own. During World War II there was a popular sentimental song called "There'll Always Be an England." It's been true for at least a thousand years now, and will no doubt remain true long into the future.

Facts at a Glance

(Note: All figures refer to England specifically unless listed as [UK], which means that they are figures for the United Kingdom as a whole).

Land and People

Official Name England (part of the United Kingdom of Great Britain and Northern Ireland).

Location southernmost portion of the island of Great Britain in the British Isles, off northwestern European mainland.

Area 50,000 square miles (93,000 square miles [UK]).

Climate Temperate.

Capital London (pop. 7.3 million).

Other Major Cities Birmingham (pop. 1 million); Leeds (720,000); Sheffield (530,000); Bradford (483,000); Liverpool (468,000); Manchester (430,800); Bristol (399,600).

Population 50.2 million (59.2 million [UK]).

Population Density 930 persons per square mile (600 persons per square mile [UK]).

Major Rivers Thames, Severn, Tyne, Trent, Mersey.

Hills and Mountains Pennines, Peak District, Cumbrian, Cheviots, Chilterns, North and South Downs.

Languages English

Religions Anglican, 43 percent; Roman Catholic, 10 percent; other Protestant and Orthodox Christian, 10 percent; Muslim, 2.6 percent; Hindu/Sikh, 1 percent; Jewish, 0.5 percent; no formal religion, 33 percent [UK].

Economy

Natural Resources Coal, crude oil, natural gas, tin, limestone.

Agricultural Products Cereals, oilseed, potatoes, vegetables, cattle, sheep, poultry, fish.

Industries Machinery and transportation equipment, electrical goods, food products, chemicals, textiles.

Services Banking, insurance, precious metals, tourism, entertainment.

Currency Pound sterling.

Government

Form of Government Constitutional Monarchy, with two legislative houses (elected House of Commons and nominated/hereditary House of Lords).

Head of State Monarch (2002: Queen Elizabeth II)

Head of Government Prime Minister (2002: Tony Blair)

Voting Rights General Election held at least once every five years. All citizens over the age of 18 eligible to vote.

History at a Glance

500,000 B.C.	First evidence of Palaeolithic (stone age) inhabitation of Great Britain.
5,000 B.C.	Rising sea levels cut off Great Britain from European mainland.
4,000 B.C.	First evidence of agriculture (Windmill Hill civilization)
2,000 B.C.	First evidence of bronze-working (Beaker People). Stonehenge constructed.
700–300 B.C.	Celtic civilization arrives in England. First evidence of iron working.
55 B.C.	Julius Caesar's Roman troops raids southern England.
43 A.D.	Emperor Claudius orders permanent occupation of England ('Britannia').
60 A.D.	Queen Boudicca unsuccessfully revolts against Roman invaders.
410 A.D.	Roman settlers in England informed that they can no longer rely on imperial protection from barbarians.
5th Century	Waves of pagan Anglo-Saxon tribes invade England. Original Romano-British inhabitants flee or assimilate. England subdivided into kingdoms (Wessex, Mercia, Northumbria).
7th Century	Anglo-Saxons converted to Christianity.
9th–10th Centuries	Vikings raid, then occupy, Northumbria.
927	Athelstan of Wessex reunites England as a single kingdom.
1066	William of Normandy claims English throne after the death of St. Edward the Confessor. His invading army kills King Harold at the Battle of Hastings.
1086	Normans compile the 'Domesday Book' recording English tax and population details.
1215	'Magna Carta', a statement of limitations of the rights of English kings, signed.
1283	Wales united with England.
13th Century	Monarch begins to call Parliaments to discuss laws and tax increases.
1337–1453	Hundred Years' War between England and France. Ends with loss of most of English royal lands in France.
1455–1485	War of the Roses between the Houses of York and Lancaster. Ends with the death of Richard III at Battle of Bosworth Field and the ascension of Henry VII of House of Tudor.
1533	Henry VIII breaks with Rome and founds Church of England.
1588	Spanish Armada unsuccessfully attempts invasion of England.

1603	James I (James VI of Scotland) succeeds to the English throne and becomes first King of Great Britain.
1607	First successful English settlement of North America (Jamestown in Virginia).
1641–1645	Civil War between forces of Charles I and Parliament. Ends with Charles' defeat and execution (1649); England becomes republic from 1649–1660.
1660	Restoration of Charles II.
1688	'Glorious Revolution' overthrows Catholic James II and invites Dutch Protestant William of Orange to throne.
1707	Act of Union between England and Scotland combines parliaments and creates United Kingdom.
1750–1850	Main years of Industrial Revolution (approximately).
1783	UK makes peace with new United States of America.
1801	Ireland, occupied by England intermittently since 12th Century, officially joins United Kingdom.
1837–1901	Reign of Queen Victoria. Sees large expansion of British Empire across South & East Asia and Africa.
1914–1918	First World War. UK emerges victorious but with grievous financial and human losses.
1939–1945	Second World War. UK again victorious, but with still greater monetary losses.
1945–1951	Labour Party Government creates Welfare State system. India becomes independent (1947) and British Empire slowly begins to unravel.
1952	Queen Elizabeth II becomes monarch.
1979–1990	Margaret Thatcher's Conservative Government reforms many aspects of British economy.
1997	Tony Blair becomes Labour Prime Minister.

Further Reading

A lot of information about England is contained within books about the United Kingdom as a whole. John Oakland's *British Civilization* (Routledge, 1995) is a good general introduction to the country and its people, as is the annually updated almanac *The Official Yearbook of the United Kingdom* (HMSO). The British government maintains a large number of useful websites, including *http://www.tendowningstreet.gov.uk* and *http://www.parliament.uk.* The Royal Family's personal website is *http://www.royal.gov.uk.* The *Penguin Guide to the Landscape of England and Wales* (Penguin, 1986) by Paul Coones & John Patten is useful for geographical descriptions. English history books run into the tens of thousands, but three especially interesting recent titles are Simon Schama's multi-volume *History of Britain* (Miramax, 2000), Peter Ackroyd's *London: The Biography* (Doubleday, 2001) and Antonia Fraser's *The Lives of the Kings and Queens of England* (University of California, 2000). *Queen and Country* by William Shawcross (Simon & Schuster, 2002) describes the life of Elizabeth II and is nicely illustrated. George Orwell's 1941 essay *The Lion and the Unicorn* is a very dated but classic description of English civilization, which can be found in many compilations. A more up-to-date description of the English way of life is Jeremy Paxman's *The English: A Portrait of a People* (Overlook, 2001). One of the best ways of getting a sense of modern England is through fiction and creative writing. Nick Hornby's *Fever Pitch* (Riverhead, 1998) is the amusing tale of a self-confessed soccer fanatic, while Helen Fielding's *Bridget Jones' Diary* (Penguin, 1999) chronicles the misadventures of a young, single career woman in London.

The Official Yearbook of the United Kingdom (HMSO, 2001).

Paul Coones & John Patten, *Penguin Guide to the Landscape of England and Wales* (Penguin, 1986)

Juliet Gardener & Neil Wenborn (eds.), *The Columbia Companion to British History* (Columbia, 1997).

Phil Lee & Rob Humphries, *The Rough Guide to England* (Rough Guides, 2000).

John Oakland, *British Civilization* (Routledge, 1995).

Jeremy Paxman *The English: A Portrait of a People* (Overlook, 2001).

Susan Allen Toth, *England for All Seasons* (Ballentine, 1998).

Robert White, *A Short History of England* (Cambridge, 1967).

Statistics from *Encyclopedia Britannica*, the *CIA World Factbook* and the *2001 New York Times Almanac*.

Index

Index

Picture Credits

ALAN ALLPORT was born in Whiston, England, and grew up in East Yorkshire. He has a Masters Degree in History from the University of Pennsylvania and is currently a Ph.D. candidate at that institution, with a special interest in 19th and 20th Century European history. He is currently working on projects connected to the social and cultural histories of the two world wars. He lives in Philadelphia.

CHARLES F. "FRITZ" GRITZNER is Distinguished Professor of Geography at South Dakota State University. He is now in his fifth decade of college teaching and research. Much of his career work has focused on geographic education. Fritz has served as both president and executive director of the National Council for Geographic Education and has received the Council's George J. Miller Award for Distinguished Service.